THE GREAT APOSTOLIC B

The Great Apostolic Blunder Machine

A Contemporary Attack Upon Christendom

JOHN R. FRY

Published in San Francisco by Harper & Row, Publishers

New York, Hagerstown, San Francisco, London

FIRST EDITION

Designed by Jim Mennick

Library of Congress Cataloging in Publication Data

Fry, John R.
THE GREAT APOSTOLIC BLUNDER MACHINE.

1. Christianity—20th century. 2. Christianity—Controversial literature. I. Title.
BR121.2.F69   1978   262'.009'04   78–3137
ISBN 0–06–063072–8

---

78 79 80 81 82 10 9 8 7 6 5 4 3 2 1

To The Champ,
Carol Alice

Contents

Introduction

The Self-Destruct Element

James Baldwin was a typical angry American Christian a decade ago.[1] He was disgusted with Christianity. He had come to see, as Malcolm X had seen, that the Christian churches were complicit in the racial oppression directed at him. He was angry about that and angry that once he had been so thrilled by the Christian message. It didn't thrill him any more. It didn't even make sense. It all seemed like a big hustle. Christianity infuriated him. But he used the great biblical theme of righteous fire to express his fury. The message in his blood raged against the comfortable-pew message in his head. Lots of Christians felt the same way.

Baldwin isn't at all like the average American Christian nowadays. He is too interested. His outrage gives him away. Bob Slocum, Joseph Heller's modern American, might come nearer to representing these contemporary folks.[2] Slocum doesn't give a damn about Christianity, and he doesn't give a damn about not giving a damn. True, he's nominally a Christian and goes to church now and then, but he goes just to humor his wife. Afterward he teases her about her preacher and the inanity of going to church. He thinks she is a conventional Christian. He laughs at her.

Although his views have been subtly shaped by Christian ideas, especially his view of evil, an official Christian idea never crosses Slocum's mind. It would never occur to him to pray, for instance. For him, as for his *Catch-22* predecessor, Yossarian, contact with the Old Plotter in the Sky is dangerous and should be avoided if at all possible.

The American Christians Bob Slocum typifies have given up on the Christian enterprise. They are not angry about it; they are not interested enough to be angry. They have concluded from their Christian experience that the only thing Christianity's God is good for is inspiring support for the churches—preferably cash. Yes, these people may be "alienated," too, even unbelievers, but above all they're bored.

An explorer of this widespread and growing boredom will eventually discover the great eschatological comedown, prefigured, for instance, in Ingmar Bergman's film, *Winter's Light.* At the close of the film, the church bell called the people to worship God. And no one came. Not even God.

Phillip Rieff has convincingly analyzed these bored "post-Christian" Americans.[3] He argues that Freudian psychoanalysis blew down the structure of Christian behavior demanded by regular official Christianity. Once that was gone, Rieff concludes, people who had been cossetted into a total world view of creation and redemption simply dropped the world view. It no longer made any sense or difference in their lives. They don't go to church or feel guilty about having stopped. They don't even think about it any longer.

Rieff is certainly right about the collapse of customary Christian behavior. He may also be right about the role Freudian psychoanalysis played in the collapse. But he misses the "self-destruct" element inside recent Christianity itself. Thousands of previously conventional Christians once went to church school; they heard the Bible preached; they had been baptized; they grew up in Christian homes in Christian towns in a Christian America. But they have dropped away. It is doubtful that they dropped away because they agreed with Freud's description of religion as obsessional neurosis. More likely they were driven out by having to listen again and again to things like John 3:16: "God so loved the world that he gave his only begotten Son that whosoever believes in him will not perish but have everlasting life." (Biblical quotations are from the REVISED STANDARD VERSION.) This sentence has caused more damage than all of Sigmund Freud put together.

John 3:16 is a short version of the total Christian message; it tells a simple story about the divine love ("For God so loved . . ."). Official Christianity tells this story about God's love in a variety of ways, often hiding it inside other stories, but always it tells it in a churchly setting. That is where the damage begins.

For the occasion of telling the story, the church is taken to be the "world" God so loved. Churchgoers are considered the inhabitants of this world. They are treated for the occasion as believer-designates ("whosoever believes . . ."); the story is told to secure their belief, even though they've heard it hundreds of times. A mild urgency is pumped into the occasion. Everlasting life hangs in the balance, it seems.

Once upon a time, the story begins, God saw the only way to get you believer-designates (in this very church where the story is being told) to believe in the divine love would be to send His Only Son[4] as the messenger. He would incarnate the message. He would be killed, of course. God could see that ahead of time. The world would kill his Son. But then the world would have to stop and think about *deicide,* wouldn't it? God allowing his Son to be killed would be a grand spectacle of Godly love all right. The grandeur would be heightened by the murder of his Son on an ignominious cross. But

God decided not to let the world have the last word. So he raised his Son from the dead.

You believer-designates were among the murderers, the story boldly asserts. Do you believe, however, that God raised his Son from the dead to secure your belief in his love? the story continues. The crucifixion–resurrection drama was enacted to secure your belief in the divine love. Yes, it is as simple as that. God wants your belief in his love; he wants believers in his church. The church tells the story. Without the church, no story; without the story, no belief. The story ends on an uncompromising note. Only those who believe *the story* get everlasting life. The others perish.

Think about it. Morally sensitive believers have, and they have stopped believing—believing in John 3:16. Something happened. It could be called modern life. The clear historical evidence is before them. It cannot be disputed. There is a believing sector of the world, which Kierkegaard called Christendom. It believes in the divine love, in John 3:16, in everlasting life, and it weeps with emotion when it hears *Jesu, Joy of Man's Desiring,* written by that great believer, J. S. Bach. There is a nonbelieving sector of the world as well. Jews, Communists, Japanese, Vietnamese, native Americans, and not a few black Americans occupy this sector. According to the story they will perish. They haven't believed. The story seems to be right, too. Millions of them did perish. Believers saw to that.

Perhaps those murdering believers had the story wrong. Many contemporary believers insist on that. They too are revolted by eager Christian support of the national war effort in Germany and America. They are revolted by mass murder. You can believe us, these contemporary believers insist. We know that God's love encompasses the entire world. But where is the assurance that now they have the story right, or ever have the story right? Perhaps the murdering believers had it right. It is a morally sensitive point, you see.

What was the divine love doing while millions of the non-believing were being killed? Just how loving a story is John 3:16 anyway? The people who believe get everlasting life. That's all they have to do: Believe. The people who do not or have not believed, or who believe something else, perish. They get something like negative divine love—the theological black hole.

That's what comes of locating John 3:16 in a churchly setting and counting churchly belief in the divine love as the basis for considering the story true. Modern history impeaches the churchly story tellers and the story itself. So, when it is retold as a grandly beautiful story within the kitsch holiness of a churchly setting, and Auschwitz or Hiroshima aren't mentioned, the morally sensitive are just naturally bored. They leave the churchly setting and John 3:16. They drop away. They aren't interested in such a story about such a God in such a church.

The morally sensitive aren't the only ones who have dropped away because of John 3:16. A lot of people have just stopped coming to church. Many of them have never thought of the matter of genocidal tendencies among believers. They have gone to atrocity-free churches filled with love-drenched Christians all their lives. They have come to see a connection between Calvary and the family potluck dinner on Friday night, the Boy Scouts on Tuesday evening, and the youth group bowling on Saturday afternoon. This apparently is the divine love in action. This is how Christians practice their fabled love. The connection between Calvary and family potluck dinners has become altogether too evident, without regard to the death of six million Jews, five million Communists in Germany and German-occupied Europe, the needless atomic destruction of Japanese cities, or incidental and more individual inhumanities disclosed in Birmingham,

Alabama, and My Lai. Some people are morally nonchalant about the relation of genocide to believing in the divine love. They are turned away by the routine tastiness of family pot-luck dinners. So this is Calvary in action, they say. It is a crashing bore.

Christianity has a self-destruct element inside itself that Rieff has missed. As Christianity's front-line representatives, preachers have to keep on preaching John 3:16 or get out of the business, even after so many believers have dropped away. Seeing these bored people leave, preachers think there is something wrong with their technique. That is why they sometimes go to the trouble of hiding John 3:16 in other stories. It is a matter of technique, they say, to make church interesting. On seeing the exodus, preachers redouble their efforts. In that they badly misunderstand boredom.

Boredom is a lot more than a specific yawning, finger-drumming lack of interest in the tritely predictable. Boredom is more than knowing ahead of time how the story comes out. These church dropouts have been bored by habitual tastelessness and by moral insensitivity. They have learned to be suspicious that what they were going to hear or see next wouldn't be quite the truth, or real, or important. It would be more like propaganda, albeit Christian. Boredom comes down to expecting propaganda. Who needs it? many say.

Christianity has gotten itself into a jam. It has itself to blame this time, and can't angrily denounce rude pagans such as Karl Marx and Sigmund Freud as the cause of its difficulty. Christianity keeps on preaching John 3:16. In this sense we can say Christianity has become a problem to itself all by itself. The problem is seen in the boredom produced by official Christian declaration, and in official Christianity's inability to comprehend that *it* is the inherent and massive problem producing all the boredom. By disposition and training official Christian thinkers, apostolic to the roots, think problems are what Christianity faces. Rude pagans, for instance. Christian history is just one victory after another over all kinds of problems, from heterodoxy to the Turks. Christianity always wins, too.

Here is what I mean. According to regular official-apostolic thinking, when people drop out of church they have dropped out of Christianity. They don't support the enterprise with their presence or their cash. The problem Christianity faces, this thinking goes, is how to survive without their presence and cash, and then how to win them back. Since official-apostolic Christianity doesn't know how to be anything else, latter-day representatives of the apostles try harder, thus aggravating the actual problem. They seem constitutionally unable to see that *they* are the problem. In their favorite move—an inspiration to our national leaders in these difficult times—they draw the wagons around in a circle. They tighten the apostolic belt. These efforts naturally end in fresh disasters of bored indifference, thus deepening the problem that official-apostolic Christianity *is*.

We all know there has been a religious revival in the past decade. How could we have missed it? Both Martin Marty and *Time* magazine confirm the fact. People are rebelieving the "old, old story" in great numbers. They also are placing mottoes such as "I Found It" on the bumpers of their automobiles. Their leaders buy expensive prime time on television in order to provoke belief within the television audience. "Believe in the Lord Jesus Christ, and send money" is the message. Conservative-evangelical Christianity is growing like a brushfire in August, we are being told. These believers are not bored. They are excited.

Don't they pump up some confidence in the Christian enterprise among the post-Christian Americans happy to have been born but once and determined to keep it that way? Hardly. Revival antics betray more of that well-known tastelessness and moral deafness for which Christianity has become notorious. "Born-again" Christians prove the point. They are the problem *squared.*

The Authoritative Representatives

I have been using the word *official* to identify a specific characteristic of Christianity. I mean by official those things the church believes that are self-evident and automatically believable. They get their authority from the church tradition and are backed up by what the initiators of the tradition claimed to be a divine authority. Christianity is most official when, in its own mind, it is representing purest second-century codifications of earliest first-century Christianity. For that reason I use the expression *official-apostolic* because official Christianity, in its own mind, must be apostolic.

The expression *official-apostolic Christianity* will be thought needlessly pejorative—by most representatives of official-apostolic Christianity. Only the severely orthodox can immediately identify themselves in the expression. Few others can. I imagine radical pastors who climbed the walls of the chancel and draped it with black crepe during the Vietnam war will be disbelieving if I call them official or apostolic. As they understand themselves, they are the true believers and representatives of the true church. They are a remnant, in fact. And they never miss an occasion to lambast the fusty old establishment church. But they are not a remnant of nothing. They believe themselves to be the truest church of all. And their true belief is not something they made up yesterday afternoon. It is the truest and best biblical theology there is, the one God revealed. They have summoned themselves up to the stature of being the *most* apostolic and official, because they think they have understood Christianity best of all. So I call them official and apostolic.

Denominational bureaucrats will certainly object to being called official, although apostolic might do. Since the mid-sixties a nascent populism in the churches has identified bureaucrats as "church officials." This populism likes to think of itself as a grass-roots movement in revolt against a domineering church establishment back East. It seems church officials had betrayed the church into the hands of left-wing ideologues. People at the grass roots didn't like that. They revolted. They tried to get their church back.

Bureaucratic uneasiness about the word *official* can be easily understood. It is a painful word. But I will go ahead and use it. I don't find denominational bureaucrats official in any officious way. They are official because they are authorized by the apostolic tradition to represent Christianity. Which they do. At least they have better apostolic credentials than the John Birch Society.

I also use official-apostolic to designate a kind of theology. It is the kind that defends the old and best faith. The framers of the "Hartford Declarations" in 1974 were standing up for the old ways and the Holy Bible, for instance. They cast themselves as essential Christian thinkers. They think that if they declare (preach) the Christian faith they have reinstated the biblical norm as a *living* authority, and the apostolic tradition of theological reflection (Paul-Augustine-Luther-Calvin-Barth) as its living home. From that position they confidently identify and abhor heresy. It is their duty to separate the theological sheep and goats.

The framers of the "Boston Affirmations" (January, 1976) thought the "Hartford Declarations" were unnecessarily conservative. The Boston group ironically chose—*had* to choose—exactly the same official tradition the Hartford group used. Harvey Cox, one of the Boston group, announced to the press, "Our main concern was to anchor social concern in the biblical message and in the central tradition of the church."[5] It was given in the apostolic Christianity the Boston group shares with the Hartford group that Cox offer such an explanation. Social concern not anchored in the biblical message and the central tradition of the church might otherwise be considered a reckless secularism and not Christian at all. The biblical message, they all know, comes from God; the central tradition of the church transmits and protects such a priceless treasure. The final advocacy of social concerns rests with God.

But the most important official-apostolic Christians are preachers. Upon their vital activity all other churchly business rests, including theological reflection. Apostolic Christianity identifies preaching as the divinely selected means for spreading Christianity. Preaching is the absolutely characteristic official Christian activity. Ten minutes after the resurrection Christianity was applying for a patent on preaching. It is Christianity's distinctive contribution to the realm of higher religion. When I use the expression official-apostolic Christianity, I mean preaching and preachers and being preached to first of all. Preachers are not the least of the officials, they are official-apostolic Christians par excellence.

There is no need to go into tedious detail in this preliminary description of official-apostolic Christianity. It is the Christianity we all know. It is the churchly air we breathe, the churchly literature we read, the Bible we study, hermeneutics, the ever-newer hermeneutics, confessions, creeds, devotional manuals, worship books, churchly magazines, churchly newspapers, brochures, fund-raising campaigns, church school materials, and pension plans. This Christianity is ponderous. It defines. It pulls its rank. It always knows everything.

As to the problem it has become: When Christian people leave, stop giving cash, or start criticizing, official-apostolic

Christianity in the name of God tries to retrieve them. It can't understand that they are in an authentic place. They are out from under the apostolic thumb, aren't they? What could be authentic about that? Feminist Christians are a dramatic instance. It is clear to them that ecclesiastical structures are sexist; so are the norms governing theological reflection on scripture; so is scripture. They often refuse to participate in the church. If they do, they gripe all the time. They criticize the sexist language of the hymns, the scripture, and the liturgy. They want to be leaders as well as followers. They ask such questions as: Women make up over half of the membership of the church, so why aren't half of the church leaders women?

Well, official-apostolic Christianity calls Feminist Christians a part of the problem. They criticize the tradition; they undermine respect for authority. They are bad apples all right. But Feminist Christians think of themselves as perfectly good apples in a rotten barrel. They are neither churched nor unchurched. They are neither apostolically and officially Christian nor quite non-Christian. And it doesn't seem to bother them. At any rate, efforts to retrieve them into the tradition without changing the churchly reality will drive them further away.

In less dramatic ways, countless Christian people have obviously stopped going along with the official program. They still believe, they say, but in different ways. They live a Christian life, but it is ordered in nonconventional ways. They may go to church occasionally or never. But this has no defining importance. With regularity they have come to associate themselves in nonecclesiastical endeavors that evoke their intelligence and sensibilities. One of their favorite words is *liberation.* They say God has liberated them from the church so that they can do God's work of liberating the oppressed from tyranny.

Within official-apostolic churchly existence, there are yet other Christian people who resist the authorities and seek drastic reform of institutional church life. Unlike those who seem to understand themselves as a remnant, these bureaucratic guerrillas aim for a humanizing of the starched authority system they see repressing vital Christian energies in the church. That they are deliberately un- , perhaps anti- , apostolic places them instantly outside routine ongoing churchly life.

Official-apostolic Christianity does not consider this growing number of former regular Christians a delight to God and an expression of Christianity. It sees their disregard of regularity as pure arrogance. It counts them as trouble. It growls about heresy. It pronounces. It throws its weight around. It expels. It anathematizes. It does not see that those very responses are a part of the problem; it sees the irregulars as the problem.

The Delicate Matter of Credentials

I contend that Christian existence is a broader and more Christian category than churchly existence. I will argue that some part of Christianity has never been apostolic or official, and isn't now. All of the churches in the world could close down tomorrow and Christianity would still be just as alive the next day. The refusal of a superannuated official-apostolic Christianity to concede such a possibility is a colossal blunder. But this blunder is only one of many. In fact I am going to call this great, fumbling, ecclesiastical juggernaut the Great Apostolic Blunder Machine.

It deserves more attention than it is likely to get these days when officials are trying to stop the confidence drain by putting on a terrific old hyperorthodox campaign, and, it seems, the churchly theological establishment is joining right in, as eager as church officials to climb out of the red and back into the black.

Look at it this way. Official-apostolic Christianity does indeed possess a critical capacity. It is called theological reflection. But theologians are employees of seminaries. The churches own the seminaries. Like oil companies, the church pays for its own expert scholarship. And it gets what it pays for. Church theologians are not exactly trustworthy critics. They are not independent. They will end up saying what the boss wants said. Since the official-apostolic church has ecclesiastical power (with fabled keys to the kingdom in its hands), whatever internal criticism it does receive from its theologian-employees is greeted with dismissal and expulsion.

Independence and critical distance from the big, everywhere-present Christianity is required if its problem, which is itself, is to be flushed out and thought about. Critical distance is my middle name. I intend to investigate how Christianity is a problem to itself and how Christianity fails to acknowledge and deal with the problem.

Before I proceed, the delicate matter of credentials had better be faced. It is delicate because for this investigation trustworthiness is so important and so hard to establish. Ordinarily, I should want to list my accomplishments as a church person. You, the reader, should be satisfied that I, the investigator, know what I am talking about. Accordingly, I should modestly let you know that I am trustworthy because I have succeeded so admirably. Pastor! Church leader! Author! Thinker! Journalist! and so on.

I am using success in Christianity as Christianity understands success, please understand, and not as its own New Testament understands success—a matter worth noting again, 130 years after Kierkegaard made exactly such a distinction. He said that ultimate Christian success, according to

the New Testament, is martyrdom. He had many a laugh
about the way the New Testament had been traduced by
Christian leaders in his time, who thought success was a
matter of opulence. It hasn't changed much in the intervening years. Success in Christianity is defined today in very
practical terms: 1) a record of advancement through the
churchly ranks from merest seminary graduate to a position
of great churchly responsibility; 2) a record of solid achievement in advancing Christianity, whether as pastor, church
leader, or churchly thinker; 3) a record of acclaim, whereby
one's achievements are widely recognized, if not in *Time*
magazine then at least in one's denominational or related
scholarly journals; 4) a record of personal integrity, which
means financial stability, marital stability, sexual stability, ex-
cellent family, fine dog, and good taste. Apostolic high-
achievers do well. They are solid and respectable. They can
be counted on.

But with the apostolic foundations crumbling, and Christianity making various moves to obscure its difficulties,
achievement in apostolic Christianity could not be considered a virtue for an investigator. In fact, apostolic high-
achievers are suspect, precisely because they might cheat—
they might defend rather than investigate. They can be
trusted to deepen the problem by trying to obscure it, if they
can be trusted at all. That is how they have become successful.

So it looks as if failure in apostolic Christianity would be the
virtue to be desired in this kind of investigation. One has *not*
shot up through the churchly ranks, for instance. One has not
advanced Christianity but has retarded it. And one has com-
piled a record of negative acclaim as a retarder of Christianity, or as a trifler with the Gospel, an ecclesiastical ne'er-do-
well. On top of which, one has a record of personal *in*-
stability; one has been known to have laughed at good taste

and has also had checks bounce. With a record of failure there is no success to protect. One can be trusted. Fine. I have failed admirably. No one could find me a worldly success, an ecclesiastical success, or a successful theological thinker. My failure is not only total, it is celebrated.

It is not naked failure that I advance as the primary evidence of my dependability as an investigator, but failure in one particular region of Christian achievement. Along with all you readers, for some time I have been looking closely at the material historical facts of the mess Christianity has gotten itself into. But I have been a failure at keeping it quiet, and this is the quintessence of failure, apostolically considered. It is so terrible it is often called *Doubt.* Apostolic Christianity demands a definite sense of realism. One must realize that achievement consists in maintaining the integrity of official Christianity no matter what one's unofficial ideas may be. If one concludes that there was no resurrection, for instance, one should mention the conclusion, if at all, to friends at a party, but never in print. Therefore, to express unofficial ideas about official Christianity, especially to publish them, is to have failed absolutely. This is the failure I gladly advance as the evidence of my trustworthiness as an investigator.

The Reverend Andrew Greeley would consider such credentials as so many sour grapes. A widely syndicated columnist, Greeley regularly maintains that people who criticize the church are almost always unable to make the grade in church. They are failures. In this he is correct. Why disguise the matter? Greeley's reasoning is that on a winners–losers scale there are inevitably going to be losers. Losers should not object to the scale itself and begin blasphemous tirades against the church. Greeley would counsel the losers to make better use of their time. They should admit their insufficiencies and get on with their business. In line with this reasoning, he advises the so-called oppressed to stop screaming and be thankful for how well-off they really are. For him the objective record of a 2000-year-old Christianity is evidence enough of its goodness, durability, and rightness. And he has succeeded in Christianity admirably; from that vantage point it will appear certain that malcontented critics are simply expressing disappointment over having failed and envy for the high-achieving church people who have succeeded.

I should like to confess immediately. Kierkegaard's description of Protestantism as "mediocrity laid end to end" rings in my ears. It is true. And I feel I am as mediocre as the next Protestant, yet I am a failure. Imagine living with the realization that one is a failure at mediocrity! It surpasses E. M. Cioran's shame for having been born a Rumanian, hence, an undeniable citizen of an undeniably second-class country. Sour grapes is hardly an adequate expression; bile would come nearer the truth. In fact, before Andrew Greeley mistakenly accuses me of mere sour grapes perhaps I should advance the theory that I am a recycling center for Christian bile—something like Christianity's gall bladder. Had I a record of failure in advertising or astrochemistry, then I might easily have adopted the posture of a victim and could have expressed something like sour grapes. But the failure I offer as my main credential has been in Christianity and particularly in something as easy as Protestantism. So it is a substantial, willful failure. It means I will not become suddenly infected with a desire to be successful after all and start to cheat. It means that you, the reader, can count on me as an investigator.

Simplicity

I don't think we shall understand the problem Christianity has become to itself if we look at its institutional complexity. That is a fata morgana. The inevitable conclusion of an analysis of bigness as such or complexity as such is predictably apostolic. Let's return to the Gospel. Kierkegaard did that magnificently in his *Attack upon Christendom*. He called institutional complexity Christendom and called it unfaithfulness too. He said Christendom didn't have anything to do with the Gospel. Poor Kierkegaard. Predictably, Christendom has lionized him. He is taught regularly in all the best seminaries. Christendom hasn't returned to the Gospel either. Had he managed to live through the ordeal of being laughed at for the wrong reason, no doubt he would have been besieged with offers to become a nightclub entertainer —the church's own Lenny Bruce.

The problem does not lie in the complexity but in the relationship of Christianity to its New Testament, the very New Testament Kierkegaard lambasted Christendom with. The problem is not complex. It is simple. Consider three interlocking Christian proclamations and see how simple it is:

☐ THE NEW TESTAMENT SAYS THE APOSTLES SAY GOD SAYS THE GOSPEL IS THE WORD OF GOD.

and

☐ THE NEW TESTAMENT SAYS THE APOSTLES SAY GOD SAYS THE CHURCH IS A DIVINE CREATION (THE BODY OF CHRIST).

and

☐ THE NEW TESTAMENT SAYS THE APOSTLES SAY GOD SAYS GOD IS LOVE.

These three intensely simple proclamations are seldom so cleanly separated; therefore, their circularity is seldom obvious. Preaching validates the church, which validates preaching, and both vouch for how well God, who created preaching and the church in the first place, is managing the universe. But there is a further circularity built into each one of the proclamations. Each is, in brief, an authority system. Each one produces belief, and belief produces Christian life. But each proclamation is interpreted as God's historical action, thereby grounding the authority system in God: the object of belief.

House theologians, moving in regions of reflective refinement well above so much simplicity, will no doubt consider these proclamations *too* simple. But I dare them to find the formulations in error. Together they define the ground for authority on one side and the ground for belief on the other side. That is the simplicity I want to isolate and describe. That is the problem. It is not lying. They are the Christian truth, after all, and Christianity does not lie. The problem is intellectual blundering. The intellectual improbability of the three proclamations is matched by an historical improbability, and both raise aching moral considerations. You already know this. I know it. Church officials know it. We know it altogether. But the proclamations are not changed. Since they are authoritatively true, authorities proclaim them *in a stronger voice,* regardless of their improbability and invincible circularity. It boils down to this. The problem is authority. Likely as not in such cases, the problem is also constipation.

At any rate, I promise to stick to the simplicity, no matter how often beguiled by comforting complexity. You can count on it.

I. THE FOOLISHNESS
OF PREACHING

1. One Way

☐ THE NEW TESTAMENT SAYS THE APOS-
TLES SAY GOD SAYS THE GOSPEL IS THE
WORD OF GOD.

This patently circular statement spins away within itself, ap-
proaching nonsense at the speed of light, until it is made
known; that is, uttered, said, proclaimed, exposed, revealed,
delivered, shown, shown off, shown forth, displayed, her-
alded—in a word, faithfully preached. Then it is true. The
witnesses are all reliable. You can take it on our word, they
all say. Furthermore, the most recent witnesses know that a
churchly witnessing chain twenty centuries long is a marvel
all by itself. Thus Christians in the twenty-first century will
be one whole century more certain. This natural procedure,
by which the faithfulness of the message and the messengers
proves the truth of the message, is the way the Great Apostolic Blunder Machine works. You know the New Testament
is the Word of God because the preacher says so. You know
preaching is the Word of God because the New Testament
says so. By expert sleight-of-hand historical origins are transformed into divine origins as though this trick weren't somehow crucial or worrisome. The move has become so auto-

matic, so self-evident, no one seems to notice or care about it any more.

It seems fated. Contemporary apostolic Christians base their preaching variously on the Bible, bibilical message, the preaching of the church, the teaching of the church, Word of God, Will of God, Jesus Christ, or the Holy Spirit. They have to. It is the routine. They follow the blundering course laid out for them by their apostolically sure predecessors. Robert Wilken, in his ingenious study, *The Myth of Christian Beginnings,* shows how the course looked in 150 A.D. to Hegisippus, a Hebrew convert who toured the Christian communities of the world and kept a diary. What he chose to put into the diaries shows him to be among the first but certainly not among the least of Christianity's great blunderers.

> Hegisippus's historical interest in lists of bishops is prompted by his concern for the unerring apostolic doctrine. He wrote his memoirs to defend orthodoxy as it was understood by him in the second century. To do this, he presents the apostles and their successors as the bearers of the true Christian faith, and he caricatures his opponents as innovators and free thinkers who have no right to the Christian inheritance.[1]

It is the same course we see right now, apostolic Christianity's "one way."

Consider contemporary preaching in U.S. churches. There we find the apostles' Bible, presented after all the intervening years as "news," a message nevertheless, a truth, something to listen to above all else, and to believe or else. There are at least eight types of preaching. But don't be misled: It is all Hegisippus, that is, Bible.

Hard Bible Preaching

Hard Bible preaching is obsessed with the totally inspired Word of God found in the King James Version of the Holy

Bible. Ephesians explains Thessalonians, which explains Daniel, which explains Revelation, which explains Ephesians. It is a fully equipped explanation system. If the modern world is ever mentioned, it is used to illustrate a point made in the Bible. The modern world does exist—it will soon be brought to an end by the Second Coming; it is also the place where the Redeemer finds lost sinners.

Hard Bible preaching makes rational assertions. It does not argue in an if—then fashion (*If* the ten commandments are true, *then* abortion is murder.); it asserts. The ten commandments are true. Abortion is murder. The sun stood still. Lazarus walked. Fellowship is the gift of the Spirit. These assertions were first made by God in the Bible to instruct believers. Bible-believing preachers faithfully pass them on. This kind of preaching does not attempt to persuade; it instructs. Christianity distinctively possesses biblical truths; preaching distinctively displays them. Hard Bible preachers formally honor the evangelical intention to declare saving truth to lost sinners. But lost sinners couldn't understand what is happening unless they had spent the last ten years in training to get saved. Saved listeners, however, do understand. Hard Bible preaching has an intimate feel. It is exclusive. Only veteran hard Bible preachees know what is going on.

This kind of preaching is capable of tough polemics. It directs its fire against other hard Bible preachers for some minor deficiency of biblical understanding, but rarely against liberals or unbelievers who haven't any biblical understanding. The latter are sometimes mentioned—as hopeless—but seldom singled out for detailed criticism. But a fellow hard Bible preacher who unfortunately doesn't appreciate the ultimate significance of anointment, let's say, will be subjected to withering critical abuse on the grounds that God has taught anointment. And God knows.

Soft Bible Preaching

Hard Bible preaching is found in local churches as much as in radio and television "ministries." Soft Bible preaching is found almost exclusively on the air. It is not totally focused on the Bible pure and simple; it believes in Adam and Eve and talking snakes, too. It is guided by softening commercial considerations. Soft Bible preaching is not satisfied with conducting a fourteen-week study of II Thessalonians; it also has an attractive study guide, which it offers to listeners at unheard-of low prices, in exactly the same way it offers salvation. The listener is not upset because God's salvation is free, but God's truth in II Thessalonians costs money. Similarly, soft Bible preaching advances a battery of special needs. First a prison ministry (of the Word), then an orphanage in Korea, or perhaps some evangelists in Mexico; the claims of the very radio and television ministries themselves are special needs. These ministries need hard Bible preaching to flourish. Soft Bible preaching needs inspired faith. But it recognizes that it needs money, too, so it sets about the task of getting money to go on—to hard Bible preaching.

Soft Bible preachers will quickly run through an obligatory piece of hard Bible preaching. With a hard-driving style they swiftly come to conclusions, in order to move on to the appeal. The "pitch" goes something like this: "God has given you [the listener] some money; God has set up this needy ministry to honor his name; if God should lay it on your heart to give some of his money back to him, then please do." At times soft Bible preachers say, "Send me your prayer requests [I am widely known to have significant prayer power given me by God]; if God moves you to add whatever you can spare into the envelope, in behalf of God who didn't spare even his own son, then fine. But don't worry if you can't spare anything. God will take care of this ministry, never fear."

There are almost no polemics in soft Bible preaching. There isn't time. There is scarcely time for the Bible. The beloved old King James Bible is always there in the background, however. It is the reason for needing money. The commercial content of soft Bible preaching is divinely authorized, and the authorization is to be found in the hard Bible.

Moral Bible Preaching (Self-Help, Self-Improvement Department)

In moral Bible preaching the accent falls on living a Godly, successful life in the modern world. The accent then falls with greater force on the Bible, which is so clairvoyantly shrewd about practical, twentieth-century, successful behavior. This preaching does not mechanically match modern situation to moral precept in the Bible, then draw conclusions. The Bible is not that kind of moral textbook. It is a divinely inspired revelation of God's practical truth. Preaching on the subject of the biblical way for men and women to be related is very clear that the biblical way means God's way. The biblical way is announced on a take it or leave it basis: God's way or some other (stupid, women's lib, gay) way. God's way is dominant male related to compliant female, as Christ is related to the church. Modern people should understand the divine basis for the biblical way and accept it for what it is. Then they are promised a bonus in the form of happiness and contentment, the wife greeting the husband wearing nothing but Saranwrap, the husband greeting the wife "manfully."

Moral Bible preaching accepts the orthodox apostolic account of everything from creation through Second Coming. It stands on that hard Bible position in order to proclaim practical down-to-earth truths about how to be happy, how to be successful, how to arrange family life, how to live creatively, or how to get the most out of life. There is a modern world here. It is the world of mummy and daddy, buddy and sis, living among other nuclear families in the moderate luxury afforded them by beneficent big business. Moral Bible preaching addresses this world, in detail, as the place to which the divinely sponsored biblical truths are connected.

Such polemics as are discovered in this kind of preaching will generally be directed against needlessly complicated versions of the modern world; those that dramatize the plight or anger of the poor, for instance. Moral Bible preaching in its polemics shows what otherwise might never be noticed: that the Bible can be trusted to present the authorized version of what the modern world *is*, as well as God's way to be happy and successful in it.

Spiritual Bible Preaching

God is a *Spirit*, you see, and thus cannot be sensed normally but can be known unnormally. The ability to know God as a Spirit defines the human being as spirit. Spiritual Bible preaching concentrates on the interspiritual relation between God and human beings. This is the fundamental biblical task: to develop the style, truth, and outcomes of that relationship. Although the official-conventional apostolic account of everything is depended on, spiritual Bible preaching seldom goes into the details of that account. Spiritual preachers will regularly bypass the gruesome business of what happened after the last supper, for instance—they will even skip the Synoptic Gospel treatments of the supper itself, and the crucifixion for that matter—in their haste to get to the spiritual revelations in the Fourth Gospel about such things as the chain of love, spiritual fellowship, union in the

Spirit, the presence of God, the peace beyond mere understanding, and everlasting life. The modern world appears in
this preaching as what human beings should pay no attention
to. Rather, they should get into and stay in a direct relation
with the patiently waiting Creator of it all. Proper interpersonal relations between human beings belong to the same
spiritual order. They should be modeled after, say, Jesus and
the disciples, Ruth and Naomi, David and Jonathan, Elijah
and Naaman, and Christ and the church.

Because spiritual Bible preaching is endlessly conflatable
with other styles, it is most often discovered in combination,
but it does exist as a kind of preaching all by itself. Spiritual
Bible preachers are staunch advocates of prayer, meditation,
love, union, peace, hope, faith, and communion. They are
advocated as spiritual experiences—the very thing the Bible
is and promotes. To be a Christian means to have these experiences; the Christian church exists as the possessor of the
spiritual book that guides Christians to these experiences. It
proclaims what these experiences are and then treats the
two-phase act of proclaiming and listening as those experiences themselves. Preaching about love followed by hearing
about love *is* love. The spiritual Bible duplicates itself on
being preached. Private meditation and private searching
(study) of the Bible, while everywhere encouraged by
spiritual Bible preaching, gets its meaning and direction
from the authoritative spiritual discourse of the preachers.

Doctrinal Bible Preaching

There is a another type of preaching, which glorifies the
Bible as the norm, authority, and everlastingly final word on
how to "do" church. The main thing on the divine mind is
the purity of church organization and church thinking. Doctrinal Bible preaching presents justification by faith as the

authoritative biblical pronouncement on what the Christian church must believe about justification by faith. Church purity, two natures–three persons, the rule of scripture, incarnation, atonement are preached as divine subject matters, first having been settled in heavenly thinking, and now waiting to be confirmed in the churchly mind by preaching. There is almost no modern world in this kind of preaching, but there is a tremendous lot of modern church. Doctrinal preachers speak of contemporary church matters in detail and at length as the targets of the divine address. God knows all about missions, evangelism, prevenient grace, premillenarial heresies, the standards of church membership, the right way to baptize, stewardship, bishops, and how to distinguish between true and false charismatics. There is no end to what God knows about these church matters. The modern ecclesiastical reality is sucked into the apostolic world as its annex, and is addressed straight on by apostolic surrogates as the very most important thing in the universe. Important thinkers in Christian history enter doctrinal Bible preaching because they have emphasized the biblical content or fundamental importance of particular doctrines. Augustine, Luther, and Calvin are examples. Montanus, Servetus, and Munzer are mentioned, of course, as examples of what happens when the doctrinal Bible is not understood or is not taken seriously. Radical thinking at best and heresy at worst are what happen.

Like hard Bible preaching, doctrinal preaching is very rational and is polemical in intention and instinct. It would gladly follow Calvin and burn contemporary Servetus-like perverters of true doctrine were the U.S. Constitution not in the way. Doctrinal Bible preaching does hate sin. Sin is bad thinking in the church about the church.

Relevant Bible Preaching

A sample of sermon titles found in relevant Bible preaching shows: Liberation and the Psalms; The Bible Speaks against Racism; The Bible and the Energy Crisis; Amos and Watergate; Jeremiah and Ecology; Isaiah and Kissinger; Jesus and the Church Bureaucracy; The Bible and the United States; The Bible and Brotherhood. These titles are obviously dated, as they should be. The biblical message should confront the modern world right now. An up-to-date sample is theoretically impossible, because relevant Bible preachers never know what crisis they'll have to confront the Bible with next Sunday.

In this kind of preaching, the heavyweight champion absolutist King James Version of the Bible in hard Bible preaching has been dissolved into a biblical message. The historical-critical disciplines of biblical scholarship are in force. Hence, the notion of literal divine inspiration has been replaced with a more vague notion that the biblical literature or the biblical materials are unique but still decisive records that reveal *how* God acts in human history. And whatever this divine activity is—saving, liberating, freeing, judging, ruling—it appears in relevant Bible preaching in a messagelike package and is immediately addressed to some perplexing feature of the modern world. How God acted "then" is a dependable ground for determining what God is doing "now." Since the divine tendencies "then" did not shift around, they may be depended on not to have shifted in the meantime. God is God.

There is a great deal of modern world in this kind of preaching, appearing as social problems, political situations, and the general interpersonal mess (families falling apart, values slipping, wife-battering, child-battering, husband-battering, and so on), about which individuals have every reason to be perplexed. But these pieces of the modern world are subtly shaped in being described. They are being readied for an upcoming solution. Racism is one of the favored subjects of relevant Bible preaching. It is presented as an ugly social-economic-political practice that God is directly and unfailingly against. The biblical message of justice says so. Before proclaiming a hot, up-to-the-minute biblical answer to racism, a preacher will first go into the biblical assessment of the damage racism produces, which modern people don't rightly understand.

The polemics of this kind of preaching are hard and heavy. Preachers go into tantrums of rage, disgust, and sarcastic fury at so-called Christians, at the flatulent Christian church, which is unrelevant, at ordinary racist-sexist Christian piety. The scorn found in this kind of preaching is based on what the relevant Bible message is, and more often than not attention is called to the great trashing prophets, or to Jesus' contempt for hypocrisy, as models for relevant Bible preachers. In this way they feature themselves as following in authoritative footsteps; they understand themselves to be representing the true Bible-within-the-Bible, and should not under any circumstances be considered as mere left-wing, activist ideologues.

Radical Bible Preaching

Relevant Bible preaching has a theoretically activist orientation. It aims to proclaim the biblical message in such a way that listeners will accept it as the truth and mend their ways accordingly, getting into social or political involvement, perhaps, as a consequence. The emphasis is on relevant biblical message. Relevant Bible preaching seldom transmutes into radical Bible preaching, although they share many characteristics and are, in fact, often confused with each other. Action is the preeminent concern for radical Bible preaching. Consider a selection of radical Bible preaching sermon topics: Jesus the Revolutionary; The Christian Basis for Socialism; God our Mother; Salvation Means Liberation; Creative Refusal; The Bible Against Itself; Christianity's Critique of Religion; Black Moses; Jesus X Christ; Vinceremos; The Death of the Patriarchal Christ. These titles have been fashioned to be provocative and controversial, and are militantly open in proclaiming a radical gospel, which is easily contrastable with the other—conservative and liberal—gospel.

Radical Bible preachers proclaim that the *Bible* insists on total and politically radical Christian involvement in the affairs of the modern world. Instead of a messagelike proclamation, they favor a summonslike or subpoenalike piece of plain lightning. "God is calling you right now to choose which side you are going to fight on: the pigs' side or God's side. Which will it be?" The radical Bible preachers' God is pure angry righteousness, demanding righteous and total Christian action. There is a hard Bible in the background of radical preaching to the extent that radical Bible preachers maintain God's rule, God's justice, God's triumph over evil, God's will to save lost humanity. What makes radical Bible preaching *radical* is the way in which the conventional Christian signs are changed so that the poor become God's elect, capitalism is anti-Christian, God is female, Jesus was black, and so on. Radical Bible preaching proclaims with all the thundering certainty of hard Bible preaching, but it proclaims something else.

There is a modern world in radical Bible preaching. It is a world full of oppression, repression, alienation; hence, racism, sexism, elitism; hence historically composed configurations of economic-political-social power which, naturally, must be resisted to the death. The energy for resistance comes from the radical Bible, as does the warrant for resistance. The radical Bible provides norms for the analysis of the modern world and makes that analysis—with the action it leads to—*authoritative*. Radical Bible preachers are not ordinary socialist, anarchist, or simply left-wing thinkers. They are *preachers* in the Christian church first of all.

Hidden Bible Preaching

There is still another biblical type of preaching, which does not much mention the Bible or dwell on its specific contents. This preaching takes the form of rational-moral discourse. Its themes may be very radical, conservative, or middle ground. It operates on assumptions of what is important to talk about in the modern world, and is similar in many respects to relevant Bible preaching. Such preachers talk, discuss, develop, explore, suspect, and explain. They are taking account of the modern world, they contend, in two ways: They are dealing with its very real problems, of course, as themes that have risen into importance; they are also taking account of modern human beings' antipathy for being preached to. They are sensible and want to think things out for themselves.

These preachers therefore junk old-fashioned proclamation. They adopt a different style. They do not tell people what must be believed. But they are proclaiming nevertheless—that this less irritating and more intelligent form of discourse is in line with the way truth is. Behind the proclamation stands a hidden Bible authorizing the proclamation. *God speaks* is the hidden item in what follows; God speaks through insight, or the dialectical movement of cognition, or some such.

Hidden Bible preaching breaks down into at least three subtypes: intellectual Bible preaching, esthetic Bible preaching, and ethical Bible preaching. In these subtypes the Bible is hidden as an actual book and becomes certain global themes, such as redemption, the structure of apocalyptic literature, the Christian view of irony, the Christian view of original sin, the cruciform nature of history—without further ado or explication of the actual mixed biblical contents from which the themes have arisen. These themes are then related to contemporary intellectual, esthetic, and ethical subject matters. These subtypes of hidden Bible preaching superficially resemble relevant Bible preaching. They are, however, notorious for not wanting to have a Bible in some polar relation with modern life; they hide the Bible in a discussion of modern life and thus assert its importance (ultimacy, truth, saving power). For instance, you can understand John Berryman's poetry when his manic humanism, describing a sine curve between extravagant love of life and extravagant despair, is found to be a defective *Christian* vision. In such a discussion the Christian vision of the relation of love and despair of life will somewhere appear. There is, then, as much Bible in these subtypes of hidden Bible preaching as in hard Bible preaching.

This classification of contemporary preaching does not take up the eccentric developments in the types and does not describe fully the conflation of types. There is a lot of conflation. And no mention is made of various highly personalized preaching styles—the use of weeping, rattlesnakes, jokes, stories, electric guitars, commercially prepared sermon outlines (for busy preachers who haven't the time to think out a sermon a week), and dialogue. Idiosyncrasy is everywhere present in this diversified contemporary preaching. But the diversity is misleading. Kathryn Kuhlman and Cecil Williams turn out to be more alike than different. Billy Graham and William Stringfellow are brother preachers after all, despite their extreme differences on every subject.

Paul Happened

A preacher appears on the horizon of Christian conscious-ness on Sunday at 11:35 A.M., an individual, who has needs; a fellow human being. But it is Word of God time. Unseen, a series of lightninglike operations have produced a startling transformation of this regular human being into a preacher. Here is what Christian consciousness is busily doing. It is recognizing that this person has been ordained to preach, after being qualified by a thorough seminary education. Without actually thinking about it, Christian consciousness knows this person has learned the Bible from reputable Bible teachers and probably knows Greek and Hebrew. This per-son is not a regular human being, Christian consciousness knows. This person is alleged to have read Karl Barth.

What is happening? Lightninglike recognitions are recy-cling this ordinary person into an apostolic authority for the occasion. Because it is 11:35 on Sunday morning, and Chris-tian consciousness is in church, and there this person is with a Bible, Christian consciousness knows that this person is a preacher. So it knows what to expect and falls into a reverent hush. After such a lot of hard work, it is now ready to hear the Word of God.

Let skeptics and other unbelievers smile suggestively as they endure preaching. They do not know. They are not in the marvelous chain of witnesses. How could they know? There seems to be a little conspiracy to keep the faith. Even Christianity's main and definitive apostle calls it foolishness. But he says it is a divinely thought-out foolishness, exactly in line with the foolishness of Christ crucified, by which the power to save is demonstrated. We are recalling the words of Paul in the New Testament—no small matter for preach-ing, since where it comes from is what it is.

In Paul's thinking God is the Greatest Preacher of All. So Christianity comes into existence and maintains itself by the preaching God does first, and the following-along preaching that apostolic servants do. Jesus was merely a badly killed Messiah until he rose from the dead with a *Proclamation.* Paul was merely a zealous Christian-killer until Jesus Christ knocked him flat on the road to Damascus with *preaching.*

The origin of Christian preaching is divine preaching, according to Paul. But the matter does not end there. Had it ended there, Christian preaching would have had the character of "God says, I say," and the preacher would have been a representative of God, God saying through the preacher's saying. That was clearly the situation with the apostles. They had the Gospel. God had given it to them directly.

Something happened.

Paul happened. An interval developed between the foolishness of preaching and the God-soaked Gospel, and into that interval crowded the apostolic experts. The formula was expanded to read, "the foolishness of preaching what the apostles call the Gospel." Inevitably Christian preaching changed from "God says, I say," to "Paul says God says, I say." The reality is now in three places: in the Gospel itself—there is something new going on because of Jesus; in the reality of God—doing the something new; and in the reality of accrediting these realities. Proclamation ever after has been possessed with a self-reflective necessity. The truth and authority of foregoing proclamation is sucked up into the proclamation itself. The Gospel becomes, first, that there is a Gospel; then it is the Gospel.

The preoccupation with the Bible in contemporary preaching has its roots in what Christian preaching is. Eventually preachers are "going on back to God" in their own minds, and in a wild variety of ways base the act of preaching on the God back there (in their minds). When preachers

stand up in public and proclaim anything at all, God is standing around in the background. This internal characteristic of
preaching leads to the situation in which preaching regularly
occurs. The beloved community sits in expectant silence. A
specially trained, divinely called, ordained herald of God
stands. It is Word of God time. That being the case, the
herald declares. Believers listen.

It is an extraordinary situation. Otherwise skeptical, sometimes cynical, and perfectly modern human beings agree to
treat this one species of human speech with complete defer-
ence. They try to believe. When they listen to commercials,
they actively expect to be deceived. They try not to believe.
They are veterans of being lied to by political leaders and
subtly manipulated by mass news presentation. They do not
believe political speech as a matter of principle. But they go
out of their way to believe preaching, which is structurally
identical with situations in which one person speaks and
many listen and in which the many go out of their way not
to believe. It is given in preaching that when the divine
surrogate speaks, the many had better believe, since that
believing is what Christianity says it is all about.

It is Word of God time. The preacher does not have to
defend the message as God's Word. Common belief has already made that assumption. The preacher will proclaim
something about these words. The proclamation will nourish
belief, perhaps clarify or enlarge it. But the proclamation
exists, from its first syllable, in direct relationship with believing. Proclamation is a declaration of what is already believed.
And if it questions belief, it does so with another, better, or
larger belief in hand.

A Christian Miniworld for the Gospel

Preaching and believing go hand in hand, as though there were no modern world out there at all. This obscurantism creates something of a problem for contemporary preaching. Walter Wink, the famous debunker of New Testament historical criticism and the darling of Neo-Fideists the nation over, can remember a time when there was no such problem.[2] Tears stream down his cheeks when he thinks of the precritical days, when the biblical world and the larger modern world were the same thing. Everybody saw angels and devils. They heard God speak actual words to them. They believed in miraculous doings. Anything they couldn't understand was a miracle. Just like the Bible. So the Bible's story was the story of their own life. Jesus rose from the dead and flew off to heaven shortly thereafter. So would they, if they believed. And if they didn't believe, they would go straight to hell.

The reason Walter Wink has tears in his eyes is that not everybody lives in a precritical world now. The contemporary world is critical. It does not believe. It resembles a New Testament scholar Walter Wink dislikes, Morton Smith. He writes books like *Jesus the Magician*.[3] He is a practical atheist. So is the modern world. It does not believe in a capricious Deity wandering in and out of causality at the divine leisure. If something happens, the modern world wants to know why it happened and will not accept an explanation that calls it a miracle or the work of God. And that's the problem.

Preaching exists within an intellectual-moral world of its own making. It is a world inside the heads of contemporary preachers; it is not the same world as the one human beings who are not Christians live in or the one Christians live in when they are not enduring what Paul described with unintended brilliance as the "foolishness of preaching." As preachers stand before congregations and proclaim on divine authority the truth—or the "news"—that "prayer changes things," it would ordinarily occur to us to consider them hopelessly religious or merely insane. And thus we wouldn't think about the heroic mental achievements that make this performance possible. Preachers may also be insane and religious for all we know, but they are primarily experts in the care and maintenance of the special, apostolically contrived, Christian world they have made and installed inside their own heads.

Most of the time, preachers live in the real public world as average, unremarkable human beings. They pay their bills and tend their hemorrhoids, the same as other human beings. The more regular the better, preachers say. This is a world full of sadness and hardships, as we all know. Fellow citizens often laugh at preachers or seem to think them sissies. Otherwise preachers have to die just like normal people. It seems a point of pride with them that they are as full of dread, alienation, and anxiety as everyone else.

But they are not regular human beings when they preach. Regular human beings in the real one-and-only public world do not preach. In fact, preachers do not preach most of the time. All week long they are busy executives. They manage the extensive affairs of their congregations. On top of that they counsel the troubled. They attend meetings. They rush here and there. And all week long, like an on-again, off-again toothache, a thought keeps crowding into their busy lives. It is an anxious thought. Sunday will soon be here again, they think. That is when preachers preach. What can I preach about this time? they ask themselves, not expecting Anyone Else to answer for them. This worry over what to preach about is a weekly ordeal. And some time during the week, most likely Saturday, and probably Saturday night, they can wait no longer. They've got to decide what to preach.

Slowly, now! Investigation is at a critical point. Let us observe a preacher as he decides. Following general custom I will assume this preacher is a male.

He does first what all writers do. He sharpens pencils. He arranges paper. He goes to the bathroom. He fixes coffee. He puts it off. But it can't be avoided. Then he does what few normal writers do. He picks up the Bible. He reads here and there, his mind wandering around, remembering what he knows about this passage and that. He is on familiar ground. What he knows is what he has read, what he has studied, what professors taught him. He can see his teachers clearly, hear their voices again. The literal feel of particular books comes to his mind. These professors, these authors, alive all this time in the dormancy of his memory, bestir themselves now. They yawn, scratch themselves, and lumber into the cone of the preacher's consciousness for the purpose of watching him work. Yes, the preacher has begun to attract an audience inside his head. He does not merely remember them in a vague way. Their voices, their writing swim up inside his head. He is a theological student again. He has authorities. They know. They know that he knows they know. He has reentered a theological world.

About once a week, when it can no longer be avoided, preachers must decide what to preach. As they decide, they slowly fade out of the real world. They begin to take up their existence in the other—sacred, biblical, theological—world, the one God rules.

Until the actual decision is made, the preacher is in between worlds, in both the ordinary real world and the extraordinary theological world. He flits back and forth. In the world God rules, the preacher's decision will be the right one, because God rules it. By definition. In the other, everyday, world, his decision could be wrong. He could pick a dumb thing to preach about, which would be uninteresting.

In this other world he wants to decide right because it is important to him, and to his professional career.

But the more he reads and thinks and remembers, the more he gets reaccustomed to this theological world. It is all coming back to me, he says. It doesn't *all* come back, of course. But the way of theological thinking comes back. He becomes a theological thinker himself, thinking the thoughts of his wise and devout teachers.

In a series of complex mental procedures, the preacher has thought himself right out of the real world and into the theological world. For the purposes of preaching, the theological world is superior on all counts to the real world he has just departed. Oh death, where is your sting now? for instance. Sin, where is your victory? It is a world full of divine justice. Providence prevails. God is great and good. Problems have solutions. Questions have answers. Grace abounds. Love is triumphant. Evil is on the run. *"Heilsgeschichte,"* he murmurs to himself. That is not a fancy cussword; it is a theological word, perhaps the consummate theological word. It means, in German, holy history. It means a lot more than that. A single-word expression, it means the history of the elect people, the grand biblical story, the peculiar way Hebrew and Christian thinkers look at any history at all, and lots more.

Now in a *frisson* our preacher, on to something, rifles the pages of the Bible, looking for it. And then he finds *It*.

> Truly I say to you, if you will have faith as a grain of mustard seed, you will say to this mountain, "move hence to yonder place," and it will move. (Matthew 17:20)

It makes perfect sense, he says within himself. He takes up a pencil and writes, "Prayer Changes Things." Obviously, he is altogether into the theological world now. Everything is *Heilsgeshcichte*. The men of God who prayed to God the living presence. Abraham, Moses, David, Elijah, the apostles. They all prayed. These very words of Jesus. In *Heilsgeschichte* what do doctors know, or physicists, or philosophers? They know critical spirit, skepticism. They know *nothing*. But our preacher does know. He knows prayer, God, holy history, faith—everything.

So now he is prepared. He is jacked up with 250 mg of apostolic benzedrine. He knows prayer changes things the same way he knows the smell of his own breath and the sight of his own eyes. Faith? He is so full of faith it sometimes spurts out on the choir. So he preaches. He runs it all out. It doesn't occur to him to *pray*, as though his own praying might lead to a change in the people's belief in prayer. He is a preacher, not a pray-er. God's saving love is God's power, which in obedience becomes known to us when we humbly ask. All true enough in the deliciously shivery, all-purpose, secret superworld of faith the preacher has just reinvented for the occasion.

When preachers proclaim to unsuspecting congregations, which were reading the Sunday paper not an hour earlier, that prayer changes things, preachers are actually irregular human beings. The more irregular the better, they say. They represent their preachers' world. Getting into the proclamative situation does not appear in the proclamation, which leads Christian congregations to be surprised and impressed at times with the enthusiasm of preaching. And, obviously, proclamation is impossible outside the special world in which it was conceived, a fact that becomes clear when the clock strikes twelve. After that, preachers reassume their regular existence in the real world where prayer changes nothing, or nothing important: not U.S. foreign policy or the frequency of children's needs to go to the bathroom when traveling.

Preaching exhibits many of the characteristics of other religious practices, such as ritual cannibalism and soul-flying.

On these grounds it can be dismissed as a superstition. On esthetic grounds it can be ignored as an exercise in bad taste. On psychological grounds preaching can be defined as obsessional neurosis, or worse. But these considerations are hardly germane. Preaching requires a superreal internal Christian world. Its proclamative contents otherwise have no reality in the real modern world, the one kicking our teeth in. That preaching requires a special superworld for its existence is then more than an elegant perversity and is connected to what preaching literally is.

Jurgen Moltmann is a preacher. So is James Cone. And Mary Daly. And Bishop Gustavo Gutierrez. And Walter Wink. Even William Hamilton.[4] They are all preachers. They reinvent the apostolically contrived world and then preach, even when they preach against it, as Mary Daly and William Hamilton do. With all their preacher colleagues in the parish ministry, these major theological figures take up existence in that special world inside *all* preachers' heads, as the necessary condition for preaching.

What otherwise are we to make of the intertrinitarian communications that occur in Moltmann's proclamation?[5] The apostles are content to proclaim what God says to the church, and through the church to human beings in general. Moltmann goes the apostles one better: He proclaims what God says to God. God places Jesus on trial, and God goes to trial. God rejects God; God judges God; God was crucified by God; death died in God as God died; and so on. Just like a preacher. Interpersonal Godly exchanges *require* a separate, intimate, totally theological world in order to be proclaimed, or climb up into mere sense.

Gustavo Gutierrez,[6] furthermore, in announcing the presence of the Lord among the poor, is not reporting something going on in an actual barrio. He has miniaturized a barrio inside his head, then he has looked on that scene and sees a

mini-Lord there, just as the Bible says, and with him the
minipower to lead the minioppressed to minifreedom—that
is, salvation. It is so triumphant it is downright thrilling. Naturally. What has triumphed is the self-sustaining proclamation
of an apostolically contrived world. There, of course, divine
promises are kept, a difference from the real world real poor
in real barrios will appreciate. But, as preachers would have
it, the poor need good news preached to them the same as
normal people.

Preachers' special interior miniworld for the Gospel is in-
termittently more real than the rotten modern world at
hand. It is more real when they preach. In the preaching it
reachieves its superreal status for apostolic faith.

The soft Bible preacher Kathryn Kuhlman was representative of all preachers in this regard. All preachers are in her
fix. She was a big-time healer. Inside her head she had something like a total biblical world where God promises that he
will heal the sick. She had enough faith, and the sick were
healed, she said. Ordinary doctors and skeptics wanted to
know what was going on, perfectly convinced of the operation of ordinary causality. But she would not even discuss the
matter in those terms. "What is causality?" she asked. For her
the major thing to be discussed was the power of God. She
wanted the doctors and skeptics to admit first that the for-
merly sick people were well, and secondly that God did the
healing. Never mind about anything else, including the em-
pirical characteristics of the healing. Naturally, skeptics in
the real one-and-only public world thought it was a very
clever cognitive game she was running on them, and some
skeptics within the church were amused that healing should
pay so well—a reflection on the opulence of Kuhlman's Pitts-
burgh-based foundation. But these suspicions were beside
the point. She exhibited the existence of the privileged world
inside her own head. Even more, she demonstrated that this

private world must always become public. She did not heal privately, then keep the matter a precious secret between herself and God. She felt the need to proclaim the meaning of the healing to every corner of television land, thus to emphasize the "real" characteristics of the miniworld where Christian faith lives. She was a chauvinist about that Christian faith of hers.

Ordinary, unofficial, unpreacherly Christianity—in the streets, pews, bars, libraries, ballparks—has a concrete, lived understanding of the remoteness of the miniworld Kathryn Kuhlman inflated with her special brand of superreality— and all her preaching mates too. Human beings in these unpreacherly settings quite appropriately ask, If God breaks through certain diseases, why not all diseases, mine for instance? This is a timid way of asking a more personal question: If God would do it for Kathryn Kuhlman, why wouldn't he do it for Aunt Lydia? She loved him too; she prayed regularly with a lot of faith and still died in agony.

We already know that preachers have an all-purpose answer to this type of question. It is the "Will of God Memorial Answer": If you want to know so much about God's will, ask God, not us. But these unpreacherly people do not have a special miniworld at their disposal. So they can't ask God without appearing foolish. They know that God does not show up in the world they know about and live in. They know this with each passing sermon.

What Does God Say?

It should be remembered that this investigation of the problem preaching has become to itself has isolated preaching from its churchly setting. Normally the church vouches for preaching and preaching returns the favor by vouching for the church. We have removed that support. We are looking at preaching without regard to the nice things the church might have to say about it. Preaching looks almost dishonest when separated that way. At this point it would be possible to conclude that preaching should be banned, the pulpits padlocked, and the entire golden-throated operation shut down. The authority for such an action could come from John Leonard's immortal words, "The closed mouth gathers no feet."[7]

But such a conclusion is not sufficiently simple. And it does not address the problem that preaching has become to itself. It ignores the problem, in fact. Rigor demands that we press on past such a temptingly complex solution, delightful though it appears, on into the problem itself.

Here is the problem neat. Christian preaching can't help itself. It can't stop being itself. It must proclaim something or other. It has to assume the position of being God's mouthpiece, but not directly, you see. God does not directly sieze preaching and inspire it with a red-hot message about right now, or use preaching to communicate a bit of "news" to the world. That is *not* the way it goes. What God says through preaching is everlastingly what the New Testament says the apostles say God says.

The problem is that the Christian truth proclaimed is the Christian truth about Christian truth. It is not the Christian truth about the realities of modern life in the real one-and-only public world. How could it be?

The solution to this problem is as simple as the problem itself. Preaching could disconnect the procedures of its much-loved proclamation. It could first disconnect the "New Testament says" from the "apostles say." Then it could disconnect the "apostles say" from "God says." What would remain? What God says. Well, stripped of tradition-hallowed supports, what *does* God say? Removed from a powerful authority structure, what do preachers say God says? What could they claim as their authority other than God and their very own experience of this divine authority?

Suddenly contemporary preaching would come to resemble the very earliest Christian preaching, before there was a scripture and apostolic experts. Then Christians just talked about what had happened. The authority for their talking was the authority of their experience in the human association of being Jesus' followers. That was all they could talk about. What else was there?

It is almost too simple to mention. The honesty gained in such a solution would balance the proclamation lost. The intricate mental efforts of creating a little biblical-theological world once a week could be devoted to thinking about the only world there is—this modern world of right now.

Preaching would be out from under the apostolic thumb, free at last. It would gain, ironically, the believability it most covets and has lost so much of lately. This would be an unforeseen bonus. Investigation discovers that the solution to the problem preaching has become to itself is accepted by preachers who can't tolerate stooging for the "apostolic others." It is a personal matter. It concerns human integrity. Later they find the bonus.

I don't find much hope that the solution will be widely embraced, for two reasons. First, Christian preaching has powerful ways of defining itself. The capacity of seminaries and theological education to imagine nonapostolic preaching is limited. We shall investigate that matter in the next chapter. Second, preachers have too little confidence in the integrity of their own experience. It is so much like the experience of people who listen to preaching. It has so little hope. Their experience is filled with loss and anxiety, anyway. In that they are perfectly modern people, not knowing which holocaust to fear most, the nuclear or the ecological. Where would be the advantage in preaching, were the preacher on the same ground as the preach*ees?* Add the extra apostolic-biblical authority and a preacher can proclaim some tremendous hope or other that God will save, so don't be anxious. Take away such an authority and the preacher is in the same boat as the preachees, which is the experience of God leaving the holocaust department in the hands of human beings. Obviously, preachers prefer that priceless apostolic advantage to their own more-or-less equivocal and rotten experience. They will not likely give it up.

2. Gonogenesis, or Teaching Preaching

Behind every preacher there is a preaching teacher, also a preacher who had a preaching teacher, also taught by a preacher, and so on; which is another way of saying that behind every preacher you will find a seminary. And behind every seminary stand 2,000 years of preaching. Seminaries teach preaching and consider the teaching a preaching in its own right.

Teaching preaching bases itself on a faithfully transmitted mass of written material amounting to over a trillion words. This is the deposit of what all the foregoing others have preached, back to the apostolic others, through them to the preapostolic Hebrew others, and eventually, of course, to the Wholly Other. Teaching preaching faithfully represents and transmits what others have said. And this total preaching (called *The Library*) has been arranged—some say arranges itself—into four fields, the well-known disciplines. They are Bible, of course, church history, systematic theology, and practical theology. Church history buffs will recognize this as the 400-year-old "theological encyclopedia."[1]

Teachers of systematic theology, for instance, transmit everything that has been written about in their field. They have an evangelical obligation to exhibit the 100 million or so words at their disposal. There is a whole language here that grows out of the core Christian vocabulary; and there are styles of operation, too. These teachers present what all the foregoing Christian thinkers have thought about theological subject matter—all intellectual giants and some of them devout. What emerges is Christianity as a reflected-on preaching—the modern process theologican Bernie Loomer and (the Blessed St.) Thomas Aquinas chatting amiably—a richly thought about, pondered, speculated over, rationally criticized, and analyzed preaching. *"They* say," teachers say, then often go on to an "I say." Thus this part of the total preaching is preached to protopreachers (or seminary students) and they learn to think about the subject matter of preaching. Systematic theology teachers shamelessly admit that their part of the whole is the most important part, but students hear that from teacher-preachers in all the fields, so they come to understand that each of the four fields is the most important. Which must be true.

Happily, the requirements of academic rigor and the demands of faithfulness are the same: to get the words of the Library into protopreachers' understanding. Once this is done, they are certified as preachers to the waiting world of the church, or, if intellectually gifted, they are allowed into the Ph.D. track and thus recognized as proto*teachers* of preaching, the most demanding preaching there is. Seminaries are the training ground for witnesses; students hear their teachers preach that they are not the Gospel truth themselves but the merest witnesses to the Gospel truth preached to them, and students then get the idea. Christianity is this great parade of witnesses witnessing to what earlier witnesses have witnessed. Students get the idea that in time they will enter the parade; it will be a solemn occasion. A great burden, too. If they don't do the job right—poof! no more Christianity. As the popular saying goes "Christianity is always one generation away from extinction; *don't let it be yours.*"

On the main point all seminaries are the same: They exist to teach preaching. They secure their charter from the Gospel, which provides them with a single aim as well, to prepare Christians for the Gospel ministry. Intrinsically, seminaries are creatures of the Gospel; historically, they are creatures of Christian churches. There is no deviation or turning in what seminaries were instituted to do. The acts of institution make that point with regularity. Union Theological Seminary and Melodyland School of Theology came into existence the same way; to this day they are exactly alike in their institution, despite being almost totally different in their contemporary understanding of themselves. Robert Lynn's as yet unpublished historical study of reform movements in U.S. theological education demonstrates that new seminaries have always kept coming into existence for just two reasons: Their founders didn't believe there was enough preparation for Gospel ministry available, or existing seminaries were doing a bad job.

Even the great university-related seminaries[2] (the divinity schools of Harvard, Yale, Chicago, Vanderbilt, and Notre Dame) were creatures of churches, as the universities themselves are. The Protestant seminaries among them were set into motion to educate Christians theologically, not because that was considered good by itself but because churches wanted well-educated (well-prepared) preachers. So from the start the concrete existence of seminaries has been maintained within the larger existence of U.S. Christian churches. Churches have founded seminaries, now pay for them, supply students as protopreachers, then hire the preachers the seminaries certify. However much seminaries may want to consider their existence within the larger scope of U.S. higher education, they cannot escape being more or less sophisticated preacher factories.

Seminaries have become a problem to themselves. But investigators of the problem would have a hard time finding it. There is a great purple funk lying like dense fog over the whole enterprise of teaching preaching. And so investigation must first deal with the funk. It seems seminaries are in some kind of trouble. It seems they don't have enough money any more. Teachers are out of sorts because they might be fired any minute in spite of having tenure. Administrators are out of sorts with these "ivory tower" teachers who can't understand how hard it is to meet a payroll. Students are wondering if they have made the right vocational choice after all; there aren't as many of them as there used to be either. This is cold comfort because seminaries are finding it difficult to place a diminished number of students in a shrinking job market. The church job market is shrinking because mainline Christian churches are no longer growing in the United States; they are either shrinking or dying.[3]

Once foundations and denominations were superbly generous sources of funds for seminaries. But the U.S. economy has recently run into some bad luck; what with depression and worldwide economic instability, based on the old demon inflation, foundations are simply poorer. They claim, however, that they would still give the money if they could determine what seminaries are good for, really. They see that seminaries are a service facility for churches, so they advise seminaries to go to their churches for money. This is cruel advice because, with the exception of the United Methodist Church and the Southern Baptist Convention, denominations have more reason to ask seminaries for money than to give some. This leaves Christians in local churches as the only source for money, *if* Grace Alone is ruled out, and It is, because seminaries have unofficially known for some time that Grace Alone never gives money.

Therefore, this one more time[4] seminaries have mounted extensive scouting expeditions into the land of wealthy Christians; there seminary scouts explain to potential givers of *major gifts* that money is needed to teach preaching the Gospel. Tears of sincerity well up in the scouts' eyes at the merest thought of the Old Rugged Cross in the Little Brown Church in the Dell that might not have a Gospel, owing to not having a preacher, owing to the seminary's not having enough money. Some of these expeditions have obviously failed. Some seminaries have closed; a very few are in fair shape; the others face continuing hard times and possibly catastrophe and ruin before the century ends.

There is a generalized, unspecified uneasiness edging toward bewilderment everywhere we look in contemporary theological education—except, of course, statements of purpose, fund-raising literature, and reports to trustees. Officially deceptive hearty assurance will be found there. Everywhere else we find an anxious but clear recognition that history has gone to the trouble of kicking seminaries out of the cozy apostolic biblical-theological world and into the real one-and-only public world, where they have to scrabble for a buck just like any other human institution.

Anxiety mounts and clarity falls to pieces at the reflex of the recognition that seminaries' teaching preaching is still locked into the apostolic world. These people are not stupid. They are theologians. They know that the four-century-old theological encyclopedia doesn't work any more. (Students say as much. So do teachers. They say It doesn't hang together.) The teachers know that the Bible has been subjected to massive historical-textual criticism for over seventy-five years. It doesn't hang together either, and only heroic rational efforts have made it seem to hold together. Yet these same people move forward with their teaching preaching as though it still makes the sense it used to and is supposed to but manifestly doesn't; as though the disaster called modern life hasn't gone off yet; as though there was no modern world beating their heads off every day. It is easy to see where the two worlds of Christian preaching came from. Preachers learned it in seminary from teachers of preaching. They are experts at the game of having history both ways.

This dankly hanging purple funk looks like low morale over survival prospects; it is more than that, however. It is also an unwillingness to face the paralyzing fact that seminaries live in two histories, and at least one of them is false.

The Solution That Is the Problem

We begin investigation beyond the generalized dis-ease with a description of the solution teaching preaching has sorrowfully discovered is such a problem. We consider first the most celebrated of Ernst Kasemann's celebrated *Essays on New Testament Themes,*[5] where the problem is still a solution. He is a master at the fascinating game seminaries play, "How To Have History Both Ways." By starting with a world famous New Testament scholar of Kasemann's stature, we can honor seminaries' concern for academic rigor. This is a sensitive point with them recently, it seems, when their faculties can no longer wear their brightly colored academic robes and hats at ceremonial occasions without inviting the cruel suspicion that they like to dress up.

In his essay "Is the Gospel Objective?" Kasemann states repeatedly that New Testament scholarship can't go back into history further than the Easter faith of the disciples. It can barely get that far because it encounters the preaching of the early church everywhere. Hence, writes Kasemann:

"The Gospels are, both in form and content, documents of primitive Christian preaching; documents, therefore, of faith in the Risen Lord and therefore also of church dogma. Here and there some material may in practice go back to an earlier stage, but in principle our Christian history begins with the Easter faith of the disciples.

Easter faith is the expression to watch. It is slippery. It sounds like some kind of convictional language. In fact, it sounds like the faith of UFO enthusiasts. But Easter faith was not proclaimed by the early church as some kind of mere convictional language. Paul says as much:

Now if Christ is preached as raised from the dead, how can some of you say that there is no resurrection of the dead? But if there is no resurrection of the dead, then Christ has not been raised; if Christ has not been raised, then our preaching is vain and your faith is vain. (I Cor. 15:12–14)

This is convictional language. But the object of the conviction is an actual Easter of some kind. Easter faith is more than mere conviction, then. It is leaning toward historical report, without quite being historical report. It is inclined toward being a historically factual statement that might read something like this: There was a dead Jesus in the tomb on a Friday afternoon and by Sunday morning he wasn't in the tomb any more.

But Easter faith always manages to miss saying just that blunt sort of thing, Kasemann says the apostles say.

The authors of the "Gospels" thought of themselves as "evangelists." There you are. Their Gospels were not written as historically accurate reports of what Jesus said and did. They are better than that; they are proclamations of *the* Gospel; so Kasemann: "The very reason why the historical facts of the life of Jesus as good as perished from the primitive

Christian message was the community's awareness that its mission was one of proclamation." This Gospel, it turns out, is more than convictional language and historical report put together. It is the *Word of God.* In this way "Easter faith," on being proclaimed, climbs up and out of being the words of excited Christian preachers about the tomb, Jesus, Sunday morning, and into the region of being what *God* says about what God did between Friday afternoon and Sunday morning.

Thus from the start there is Gospel as the content and conviction of Christian preachers—your average New Testament—and Gospel as Word of God, which is somehow in but always more than and superior to the New Testament. This second Gospel is what one hears in Christian preaching that is not exactly the bare preaching. Listen to Kasemann on this point:

> The Bible is neither the Word of God in an objective sense nor a doctrinal system, but the deposit left by the history of the preaching of primitive Christianity. . . . We cannot simply accept a dogma or a system of doctrine but we are placed in a situation vis à vis Scripture which is, at the same time and inescapably, both responsibility and freedom. Only to such an attitude can the Word of God reveal itself in Scripture; and that Word, as bibilical criticism makes plain, has no existence in the realm of the objective—i.e., outside our act of decision.

The circle is complete. Faithful disciples preach that what they are saying is God's saying. Kasemann, as a recent preacher, uses New Testament language to go beyond the New Testament. He says, with a faithful flamboyance that almost takes the breath away:

> It is only through the Holy Spirit that we are enabled to come to Christ and to believe in him as Lord. And that in turn means to

hear and to decide to obey the Word as preached, as only the individual can hear and decide, and as he must always be hearing and deciding afresh.

This is a brilliant display of how to have history both ways. There is first an undeniable New Testament. It exists, as preaching. It was not composed by humorists in the third century. And it preaches about a something God says happened in connection with Jesus, which is history the other way and *more* undeniable than the preaching. This history gains its ultraundeniability because the disciples were *eye witnesses*.

Bluntly, Jesus did *not* arise out of the ground, display himself to awe-struck disciples, then fly off to heaven just after telling them in a commanding tone:

> All authority in heaven and on earth has been given to me. Go therefore and make disciples of all nations, baptizing them in the name of the Father and of the Son and of the Holy Spirit, teaching them to observe all that I have commanded you. (Matthew 28:-19–20)

That is only preaching. That is what we don't believe as *history*. We believe the preaching is history. According to the same preaching, however, God says he did something totally cosmic—totally *gracious*—in Jesus Christ, and we do certainly believe that as history. The same New Testament is the source for understanding what we don't believe and what we do believe, and it provides the authoritative norm for making these delicate arbitrations. Thus the New Testament is authoritative for what we do believe about what we don't believe and is authoritative, moreover, because the people who gave us the New Testament were eye witnesses of what *didn't* happen.

Kasemann made teaching preaching safe for the world by building on an historical-looking annex to plain old history.

This annex is the apostolically guaranteed world of proclamation. Since it looks historical enough, it can be treated by preachers as a dependable—but more, authoritatively dependable—base on which to build everything else: morals, church, group discussion, theology, stewardship, potluck suppers, sensitivity marathons, and pastoral counseling. It looks like a brilliant bit of prekerygmatic manuevering on the high-wire. Preaching teachers do the same thing all the time, although with less style, because it *must* be done. Teaching preaching requires it.

Now to the more interesting development. How is God related to the modern world? We catch Kasemann at his best in this other kerygmatic feat. He summarizes the Gospel in two ways. First, "In Jesus the divine love has taken the field and showed itself to be a life-giving power." Next, the Gospel is "The event of the justification of the sinner." Love-starved, sinful people in the modern world will recognize both of these statements as some substantial good news about their lives. The divine love is still *in the field;* sinners are still *justified,* without deserving it in the least. This is an up-to-the-minute Gospel about an up-to-the-minute God who is still active in the field. How do we know?

Kasemann's answer is clear. When, in the attitude of responsibility and freedom, we listen to the preached Gospel, we meet this love and justification. The essence of the Gospel will be found not in the bare Gospel or in the attitude of faithful attendance on the preached Gospel. The grace of God turns preaching about then into preaching about now. In this Kasemann follows Paul directly, as did Luther and Augustine. With Paul preachers correctly and modestly confess, "What I say is foolishness." Then they add, "But by the grace of God what I say is the Gospel unto salvation." The very enterprise of teaching preaching is right there with Kasemann, who is with Paul. There is always a statement of something that the Gospel *is* that grace makes clear in preaching. And this something always turns out to be a paraphrase of the New Testament or a restatement of a New Testament theme. There is a divine override on the cheerless garrulity called preaching: It is grace. And it is always what modern life doesn't deserve or expect. Grace, when not making preaching possible, is acting the part of the preached about. Grace is Tillich's New Being, Barth's Humanity of God, and Bultmann's Openness Toward the Future rolled into one. Grace is how to have Paul and modern life.

This classical-conventional and celebrated thinking of Ernst Kasemann represents the cohesion there once was in teaching preaching and how it understood itself. The modern world exists in this thinking as a demand for intellectual rigor. It is because of the modern world, for instance, that Christians recognize and identify legendary materials in their Bible. And there is a modern world full of sin and waiting for grace, that is, an abstract and biblicized modern world. On occasion this world exhibits injustice—just the thing for divine justice to overcome graciously.

Teaching preaching had an assured Gospel for a modern world in which it made sense. Everything was working out all right for *seminaries,* along the lines of Romans 8:28: "We know that in everything God works for good with those who love him, who are called according to his purpose." Furthermore, preachers went from well-off seminaries to preach in churches that were also getting along fine. The enterprise of teaching preaching, then the preaching too, fit into their own picture; Kasemann's other history made perfectly good sense, as any fool could plainly see: Whom God loves, God takes care of.

In Part II I will discuss the institutionalized presence of grace in God-given Christian affluence as "Yahoo Calvinism." It can be pointed out here that once upon a time grace had a concrete meaning. Christians were actually getting more than they deserved (as sinners), but getting exactly what the Gospel promised. Quantifiable grace (oil wells, foreign policy victories, a rising Dow-Jones, munificent suburban living) was always the extra-biblical guarantee and certification of teaching preaching. It was present in such consistent, dependable measure that it didn't have to be recognized or commented on. The God of providence and election was doing the divine business all right, as teachers of preaching could see, and *that* furnished a literal guarantee for the still coherent apostolic-theological account of everything.

Investigation now discovers that the problem seminaries have become to themselves is that very assured, triumphal, comprehensive, systematic apostolic coherence (God says, the apostles say, Augustine says, Barth says, I say) that had functioned so long with effortless ease. The solution became the problem. And investigation discovers that the problem has emerged as just that teaching preaching itself, that is, as seminaries.

Seminaries are institutions; they are more than the community of existing faculty, administration, and student body. A seminary community, any seminary community, is far more than the entire existing membership of the community; it is also trustees and the entire corps of alumni; it is the seminary plant and its maintenance; it is the decisions predecessors made to locate the plant where it is; it is its own institution and its founders' purposes; it is the Christian givers whose money paid for everything, and the money itself. Seen in this way, seminaries have specific historical trajectories that are not easily deflected. Seminaries try to become what they used to be. They are willful about it. They are stubborn.

As institutions seminaries are always enduring into the

future, adjusting, modifying, changing, as new situations demand. But they have their charter in the Gospel. They have
a peculiar view of the future. They believe it will be a
"graced" future; it will be in God's hands; it will be continu-
ous with the past. What looks like institutional stubbornness
or mere conservatism (of the sort normally found in banks or
the Mafia) is actually an expression of the Gospel in the case
of seminaries. Participants in the membership of the existing
seminary community are obliged to continue including their
own future in their own teaching preaching.

When the future toward which seminaries conventionally
endure is full of catastrophic portent, and ruin may be
around the next corner, the embodied obligation to teach
preaching a Gospel concerning a graced future becomes absurd. That is one part of the problem seminaries have become to themselves. It exists as a dirty suspicion, nowhere
rigorously pursued, of course, that the faith of the Gospel is
mistaken. Rigor would insist on a clearer reading, no matter
how absurd. Under the lash of their much loved rigor, seminaries would preach the Gospel as still true, still God's word.
But they would preach that God has *stopped* loving seminaries and has *stopped* giving them what they don't deserve. He
has started giving them something else, something like what
they do deserve—another, absurd, grace perhaps. But instead of rigorously preaching the Gospel, seminaries continue to endure into a disastrous modern life with a preaching that isn't coherent with their own concrete modern
experience.

Rubbery Rationalism

The other part of the problem has burst out upon seminaries in the past twenty years. Members of seminary communities have questioned the whole preaching being taught. They

looked at the cardinal proclamation (The New Testament says the apostles say God says the Gospel is the Word of God) and themselves said, "Says who?" There the seminaries were. The preaching—the Library—was a readily available and historically full mass of material, ready to be transmitted to the next entering class. Some teachers and some students came at this preaching with a devastating series of questions. They said that the whole Library was resting on the quicksand of an Easter faith. And they didn't let up because it was a delicate subject. As bona fide Christians these people began to ask questions about the realities in the Kasemann memorial historical annex of superhistory. These are largely phenomenologically inspired inquiries.[6]

To what realities do the bare words, *God, grace, resurrection, Word of God* refer? In what ways can these realities be known, or in what ways do they make themselves known? The conventional apostolic account *preaches* that these realities are there all right in the (super) history available to Christian faith, but what does *there* mean? In brief, where? A careful analysis of the world of the apostles does not vindicate the devout conclusions of Kasemann. It shows his piety in reaffirming the contours of the apostolic world. Belief "into" proclaimed realities can never be more than that. The realities are squarely in the proclamation, which, the proclamation insists, exist in the annexed zone just beyond history. But there is no way proclamation can *make* them exist there, so they exist there as realities for belief. They stubbornly remain in proclamation.

This analysis forces teaching preaching (painfully) to operate in one history at a time. If in our human history, then realities are *there* in some place or other, with an ID card, dates, bad breath, and a history of how they got there. If *there* means anything, realities *there* can be checked out. Anybody, in principle, can have a look. If in God's history, then realities are *not there* in our plain old human history. They exist in a historylike-looking history that does not have *theres* at all.

In such fashion the procedures of the inquiry lead to thoroughgoing desupernaturalization of biblical contents. This is not so bad. Biblical criticism has already done that. But they also lead to a more drastic descripturalization. Inevitably, the Bible exists as not-God's word. The inevitability lies in the Bible, which disqualifies itself as scripture.

This inquiry assaults the biblical bases for teaching preaching and explodes the theoretical certainty of the "Paul says, God says, I say" procession. It is no longer certain that God said anything. The apostolic formulations are equivocal at the critical point.

Concurrent with this inquiry there has arisen another series of questions addressed to the historical-*moral* coherence of the preaching.

Gradually, baptized, Bible-believing, but nonwhite Christians noticed a concrete bias against colored people in the apostolically contrived world and 2,000 years of preaching about it. These Christians were sometimes teachers of preaching and sometimes protopreachers. Their own experience rose up and smote them with that recognition. They discovered a regionalized grace, one grace for white people, one grace for colored people. Obviously, both the New Testament as preaching and the New Testament as Word of God are, most charitably put, misspoken on this subject. It is easy to see how the apostles, as ordinary culture-bound mortals like us, could misspeak on racial matters. But they are the very men who know all there is to know about God's speaking, and *they* say God said the racial prejudice. So, one way or another, God is wrong or the apostles are wrong about God on the matter of races—and grace. So said nonwhite Christians from the unassailable position of their own Christian experience. And if wrong on race and grace, then probably wrong on other things as well.

And eventually, baptized, Bible-believing, female Christians noticed something like a total patriarchal conspiracy against women in the apostolic world, and according to the apostles, in the courts of the Almighty, and according to the Almighty, in creation itself. The experience of these female Christians led them to challenge the entire patriarchal arrangement along these lines: You apostolic men say the apostles say that God says women were created to be men's helpers, to keep those knees *up*, and when in church to *shut* up. We do not believe it. And our belief is as good as yours.

The only defense possible is to admit apostolic bias against female Christians and set about rescuing everything else the apostles did not express bias against, such as resurrection, love, justification by faith, Word of God, and, above all else, grace—which women critics were certainly not showing a lot of. But how could the defense proceed? The inner criterion for distinguishing Gospel from at times misspeaking scripture is the criterion of apostolic authority: to proclaim the self-authenticating but authoritative Gospel. That is the criterion female Christians impeached, without ceasing to be Christians for a moment.

And eventually colored and female Christians, joined by politically aroused colleagues, teachers and students alike, began to point out the authority situation neat; they called it a piece of elitism. They looked at the parade of witnesses as a transmission of authority to declare what is authoritative. They looked further and found the parade dominated by white males with good university educations and academic inclinations—at least after 500 A.D., before which the elite hadn't really gotten itself together. This sort of recognition raises the authority question in a drastic way. If the elite says at this point that God calls the apostles and all their successors, then a divine favoritism for bright, Western, white males is established a priori. If the elite says that things have simply worked out this way, then the self-sustaining power characteristic of the elite is established a priori and the divine authority question is moot: There is no divine authority there; it is all ecclesiastical authority.

Were seminaries only their present members and not also their predecessors, then the entire enterprise of teaching preaching could not have sustained the shock of these three epic critiques, coming as they have in the midst of exploding bombs thrown by phenomenological buccaneers. The logic of the intellectual critique plus the force of the historical-moral critiques has been deadly. The critiques, we must note, *solved the problem.* They forcibly disconnected the "New Testament says" and the "apostles say" from "God says" in the cardinal official-apostolic proclamation. The critiques made preaching safe again and believable once more. Providentially, some would say, the communities of concern out of which the critiques arose were actual instances of post-apostolic Christianity that seminaries might become. In losing their lives as apostolic stand-ins, they might gain their lives as contemporary Christians, as their Lord precociously advised them to do. Having found it, investigation would do well to look at the solution seminaries refused.

In most cases the communities of concern out of which the critiques arose, and keep on arising, are national in makeup. The women's liberation movement is such a community. The black power movement is another. The Asian power and Chicano power movements are others. The gay power movement is the latest. In some cases, however, they are local do-it-yourself communities inside the seminaries; sometimes they are only individuals. In a few cases there are not even these individuals, owing to their having been recently fired or expelled. But in all cases seminaries have not learned of the critiques in the newspapers, they have been delivered first hand, from a distance of half a foot, by indismissible and gesticulating seminary Christians.

The phenomenon before our eyes is a clear piece of post-apostolic Christianity, living, arguing, defying, and carrying on in unmistakably postapostolic ways. These people do not preach to each other and they do not preach in their controversial confrontations with nonplussed and tenured believers in the "old way." Since postapostolic Christians do not have any authority other than the authority of their own lived experience, they do not have a background of authority for proclaiming something or other. They do not preach or believe in what is traditionally defined as preaching. They have meetings; they often call these meetings parties. That is all they have. They are forever going to or coming from a "rap" of some kind. In these meetings they argue incessantly. They place great value in being able to analyze things to the roots and a greater value on refining analysis in the open air of public meetings. Although they haven't structured their values, they do believe that their very human association, whether in the living room or the dean's office, their concerted thinking and acting, is the core of their power and their core of value. They will say, for instance, sisterhood is powerful, or Asian is powerful, or black is powerful, or gay is powerful. Mixed up with these assertions is a definite "apprehension"[7] that there is Another Power at work in their human association, which they do not feel comfortable discussing, since they can't analyze the two mixed-up powers separately.

The existence of these examples of postapostolic Christianity is set within an existence of other communities of similar concern and not in the wider existence of Christian churches or even higher education. They may or may not claim fellowship with Jesus and the prophetic revolution. The feminist theologian Mary Daly refuses to count herself a Christian theologian on both counts. In her mind she isn't a Christian as her teaching colleagues are, and she isn't a part of the parade of distinguished male preacher thinkers whose leader is Paul. Quite definitely not. She identifies herself strictly within the community that is beyond, underneath, or on top of—laughing at—Christian theology.[8]

Postapostolic Christianity as it exists in seminaries dramatically lives as though the sexual and political traditions of monogamous, heterosexual, and authority-loving Christian ethics carries no weight. Whatsoever! "What could Paul have to tell me that I could believe?" they ask. As they look at it, the truth about sexuality as well as the truth about politics should be hammered out in wide-open public settings where all secret authorities can be identified and where positions must be defined and then defended on their merits, in one history at a time.

Above all, postapostolic Christianity is convinced that seminaries should simply stop teaching preaching and delivering certified preachers to waiting churches, thus keeping the whole procession going. What could seminaries teach if not preaching? Investigation suggests this partial list of subject matters. It has variously been proposed that seminaries could teach:

parties	dancing
Bokonism	singing
how to live in egalitarian communities without frowning all the time	how to deal with a Heilbroner agenda before it is too late
theological thinking about now, not then	how to survive in religion without tenure

prescriptural Christianity	preapostolic Christianity
the history of heresies	the politics of coalition
how to spend Sunday mornings instead of the other way	how to approach a religious publisher with delicate manuscripts
what to do in jail	Ernst Troeltsch (everything)
reality-analysis	consciousness-analysis
prescriptural Yahwism	phenomenology
the history of slavery after 1864	the feminist Bible
Erving Goffman (everything)	Hannah Arendt (everything)
the politics of food	the politics of oil
peasant existence—prehistorical, historical, contemporary	how to shout in public without being accused of preaching
how to buy books with food stamps	the lives of the saints

Such a partial but provocative list summarizes the subject matter that is advanced regularly by postapostolic Christianity as post–teaching preaching. The subject matter is naturally related to the further expansion and development of postapostolic Christian existence. It has not been drawn up with reference to preparing Christians for something else, such as churchly existence. There is something compelling here. Seminaries can see that. The phenomenon is fascinating because it is so clearly beyond the problem seminaries are. But then seminaries are more than their contemporary recognitions and fascinations, more than their perfectly sound experience of general apostolic collapse. They are also and decisively the latest representatives in a distinguished parade of apostolic surrogates and descendants. As institutions within churchly existence, seminaries just naturally have not accepted the force of the three epic critiques or

admitted the existence of their phenomenological question-
ers. Instead, seminaries have rejected what might be called
their divinely appointed "new life."

In fact, teaching preaching has treated the three critiques
as an institutional inconvenience. They have adjusted; they
have added a dean here, a professor there; changed this
procedure; done that. Seminaries have not been paralyzed,
they have been galvanized into counterattack. Powerful
figures from the past have awakened and made their presence known. Founders have arisen to demand action. Promi-
nent thinkers have wrathfully taken the field to confront this
disconcerting insolence—which has, of course, deepened the
problem, since to the raw problem must now be added "bad
faith."

Although radically challenged, teaching preaching has not
admitted that the critiques in the least disturb the apostles,
who, by the way, counsel grace and forgiveness and wisely
leave judgment in the hands of God. The theological response has hardly been elevated. It has had about it the feel
of a sort of rubbery rationalism, as when Christian ethicist
Paul Ramsey tutors feminists on essential portable natural
law, or Christian ethicist Paul Lehmann counsels his black
friends on the progress of revolution, or Bible teachers
scramble for position in explaining away such a mass of sexist,
racist, and elitist language in their field. The activity of teaching preaching was brought into sharpest question; teachers
of preaching reacted by bringing the critics into sharper
question. The basic all-purpose response, Calvin's response,
by the way, learned from Augustine, who learned it from
Paul, was: Here you sassy know-nothings come before the
altar of theological reason with your impudence. Well, "Who
are you, O man, to answer back to God" (Romans 9:20). They
said: The gender of God is not even an interesting subject;
he has no gender. They said: Dispute over the color of God

is frivolous; God is no-color. They said: The dynamic for inter-racial understanding comes straight out of the New Testa-ment. For every Romans 13 there is a Revelation 13. They defended, parried, trivialized, changed the subject, and did everything but admit the historical-moral point and deal with the intellectual point, which was that, in all their ma-neuvering, they were *preaching*. And the Gospel they preached was . . . rubbery rationalism.

E. M. Cioran advances the elegant conceit that Christian-ity tremendously limited its theological possibilities when it expelled the last great polytheists from the church in the second century.[9] He sees advantages in polytheism, and he would be encouraged to believe that official Christianity has indeed developed its first post-Gnostic polytheism had he first-hand knowledge of these recent seminary responses. It seems there is first "God"; this is the one who has no gender. Then there is "Grace," whose function as a deity seems to be associated with calming everybody down; then there is "Yah-weh," who is definitely Jewish and *not-white*. He can stand for black, brown, red, and tan Gods, whose existence is so far merely alleged by certain fanatics. There is also "Jesus Christ," the Transcendent Reality of an indeterminate, mixed gender, and "Jesus Christ the Son," who does have a gender. There is "God Almighty," the Ruler; there is "Holy Spirit," a fluttery feminine deity but not female at all. Finally, there is "One God." This is the God to be relied upon when the suspicion of polytheism is mentioned.

These many Gods populate the region of response to the three critiques. They play different divine roles and alto-gether form what rubbery rationalism understands the di-vine universe to be. Headlong and terrified retreat into a Wholly Sacred world could have been easily predicted, given the racket and rampaging of enraged seminary predecessors, but not this unexpected leap into polytheism. But, we note, for all the versatility theology gains, it loses something too: It loses class.

Some Good News

Seminaries are a worse problem than ever just by continuing to be what they are. But in enduring into the calamitous inquiries, critiques, assaults, explosions of their very apostolic world, seminaries have definitely moved beyond where they used to be. It is by way of Bokononist analysis that this discovery can be documented. Bokononism is a religion described and advocated by Kurt Vonnegut, Jr. in *Cat's Cradle*.[10]

Bokononists believe, as does apostolic Christianity, that God does not care for the poor and the colored, or for women either, unless with knees up for the making or delivering of babies. God has it in for these people. The evidence for this belief is in human experience and it is overwhelming. Indeed, God rules the world and has designed a peculiarly malevolent destiny for 80 percent of human kind—a fact that cannot be disputed, least of all by the 80 percent. And Bokonists believe, along with apostolic Christianity, that God selects and uses the 20 percent in arcane ways, to effect ends very distant from their apparent purpose. A Wise Providence is also cunning. Most of the ends are whimsical and finally can be seen only as some divine mischief or other. When Bokonists run into bad luck, they say, "Busy, busy, busy," because they suppose God's mysterious purposes are being worked. They never try to excuse God. They believe earnestly and totally in God; they believe the worst all the time. And so in Bokononist analysis of apostolic Christianity, which it so much resembles, bad luck is bad *grace* because Christianity is notorious for believing only the best of God. But having conceded that, what can be made of the apostolic insistence that what is so clearly before the eyes as bad grace is not instantly understood to be the work of God? Isn't God still the *Ruler?*

Why weren't seminaries able to admit straight out that the God of the apostles does not like the poor, colored, and female? What is wrong with that—the truth? Why couldn't they recognize that the Ruler of Everything has not lost control or changed divine policy? He simply doesn't care for that class of people, and he never did. Closer to home, when seminaries came upon bad grace, why didn't they instantly connect it to God? Whatever happens is God's work, isn't it? Bokononists think Christianity is a peculiar religion, and they offer friendly counsel to Christianity. Always *watch out* for the Great Plotter in the Sky, because he is powerful and up to no good. Christians who believe God is powerful are always watching out for mercy and forgiveness. When the historical evidence is very plain that churchly existence has been reclassified by God and placed in the colored and female region of the world, why can't apostolic Christianity believe its eyes, see bad grace, and begin to watch out? With such a recognition seminaries might begin realistically to estimate their chances, as though they were colored and female too.

Bokononists take God seriously, because they have no illusions about his power. Teaching preaching, which believes the same thing, has heretofore connected God to a certain selected area of experience. Teaching preaching hasn't had the occasion to look at the apostolic world with Ruler God and all kinds of power from the standpoint of being on the ground, stood *on,* with a divine foot in the face. From that position God's world admittedly looks different; God looks different; so does grace; so does providence.

Having rejected the solution that postapostolic Christianity offered, seminaries should face the music. That is the Bokononist recommendation, in fact: Be brave, now that you have run across some bad grace. Take the standpoint of Jews just as they sailed into a Nazi oven. There is bad grace for you. In just the moment of sailing, they had the direct intuition (almost overpowering) that God didn't want to lift a finger to arrest the flight. These Jews didn't doubt God *could* do something; they just knew he *wouldn't*. Fine. From such a standpoint apostolic Christianity can continue to believe in its God, and will be occupying the place almost everyone else always has.

But then, teaching preaching has not made such a clear theological description of its contemporary situation. Investigation concludes that seminaries either do not believe in God at all, *or* they have begun to move away from and beyond the whole preached apostolic world. In either case they are still a problem to themselves, but at least they are no longer *serious* apostolic Christians, and that may just turn out to be some good news.

II. THE LOCAL FRANCHISE

"If it doesn't happen on the local level, it doesn't happen."
PAUL CALVIN PAYNE

3. Church Swamping Church

☐ THE NEW TESTAMENT SAYS THE APOS-
TLES SAY GOD SAYS THE CHURCH IS A
DIVINE CREATION (THE BODY OF
CHRIST).

The New Testament says other things as well. The church is the people of God, for instance, at times a holy people, a community of faith, a covenant community, even the resurrection community. But *the body of Christ* is its favorite phrase. It best presents Christ as the head of the church. Whatever term is used, the church is never anything less than a divinely proclaimed reality with a divine origin. The church, of course, wrote the New Testament.

A largely invisible reality, the church exists in the mind of God, sometimes specifically in the mind of Christ. God alone knows the full extent of its membership, since the choice and selection of the members is God's work. It is an invisible and transcendent reality—"the communion of saints"—collected and held in the divine purpose. But the church is not altogether invisible. What use would that be? The way the church sees itself, it is a visible collection of believers. It is located somewhere. It is located in many wheres. Take them all together and you have *the* church. It did not spring out of the mind of God at Pentecost as a full-blown worldwide reality. It started, the apostles proclaim, at Pentecost as the church in Jerusalem. It had a perfectly localized origin. The church then spread to other localities. That is how it works. It spreads from here to there.

The church provincializes itself. It has to. In that way it gets into concrete history. Whoever heard of Jesus of Earth, or Jesus of Galaxy? Jesus of Nazareth is the way to say it. The church of Corinth, or Biloxi, Mississippi. God intends the Gospel to be preached, believed, and spread through the agencies of the churches within other living historical communities. We are not a movement, they say. God could have used schools or the army, they say. God could have done his will by way of angels exclusively, they say. But he decided on the church and in the process specifically rejected a corrupt Temple-Judaism. God asked: How shall I concretize, transmit, and universalize the good news of my love? He answered: the local church. And God knows.

Knowing what God knows, the church cozies itself down somewhere for the purpose of being what it is. While it would be nonsense for the church to say it is at home in the world —because the church says its home is in heaven—it would be more nonsense to ignore its home in Ashtabula, Ohio as the Second Methodist Church. Investigation finds the body of Christ in places just that local. *It* is the body of Christ. The people of God there will be only too happy to trace their origin backward through circuit riders, revivalists, lay preachers, Wesley, Reformed Episcopal bishops, on back through the apostles to Jesus Christ, and God. Something happened at Pentecost. God started the church. God went down to the apostles. They went out to the world. Presto!

here we are, these Ashtabulans will say. And that is how the Glorious Apostolic Blunder Machine works.

We are looking at the origin of the church from an admittedly unusual angle. Official Christian commentators would likely call it perverse. We have ignored preaching, just as we ignored the church. It *is* an unusual angle. Customarily we find the origin of the church propped up with about four million of the choicest words of preaching. Preaching has *its* origin with the Greatest Preacher of All. So it can be believed when preaching says, "The New Testament says the apostles say God says the church is a divine creation," because that is the word of God. By definition. Now investigation finds the church saying, "The New Testament says the apostles say God says the Gospel is the word of God," and the church is after all a divine creation. This is camouflage. The church will go to any length to be regarded as a divine creation. Investigation cannot decide between treating these procedures as comical or as dishonest. In the church's mind, however, they are simply true. And this pleasant little insistence has gotten the church into the trouble it's in right now.

Apostolic Christianity is churchly existence. It comes down to and glories in being some Second Methodist Church of Ashtabula. It would be uncomfortable as Bill's Bar or as the Ashtabula Community College. It is a church. It has a mission. The mission is to convert Ashtabula to Christianity. The church could not do that as Bill's Bar, the church thinks, or as a college either. The church has to be a church.

Churchly existence, no matter how comfortably settled in some other local existence, is uneasy if it is not growing. It has a fanatical desire to reproduce itself. This desire amounts almost to an Instinct. It is called *evangelism*. The church wants to get everybody to believe what it believes and, of course, to get everybody to join the church. This can take two forms.

In the main form the church simply cuts out all the monkey business and preaches, flat-out, to unbelievers. It says to the unbelievers, you people are sinners and you are going straight to hell if you don't believe what we believe (and join our church). In the other form, the church cuts out the preaching and lives a godly life. In H. Richard Niebuhr's five types of church–culture relationships,[1] this type of evangelism would be called Church Transforming Culture. (The main type would be called Church Converting Culture.) The idea here is that godly living will be an example to the unbelievers. They will see all of this love and say Wow! I want some of *that*. They themselves will begin living the way they see the churchly examples living. The unbelievers might in time actually join up, too.

The people of God rightly note they wouldn't be members if someone hadn't preached to them, or to their parents at least. So they are restless if they are not doing the same thing to the people who are not yet the people of God. The church that isn't growing is not doing its job. By definition. Churchly existence is not only local, it is forever trying to become totally local all the time.

In its understanding the church has come out of the divine mind. What comes out, however, is eminently sensible. Exactly what a sensible God would think up. Along with its divine origin, the church has a poignantly historical origin as well—within the divine origin. It fits sensibly into the expansion of Christianity in a specific way. Perhaps seventy-five years ago some people of God at the First Methodist Church decided God was calling them to fight for the purity of evangelical Christianity. They lost the fight, but they didn't give up their zeal. They left. They started a new church. This very church. Present members have two reasons to be thankful: for Pentecost and for fighting predecessors. This double origin is as it should be. As it *must* be. God started *the* church and *this very* church.

Accordingly, contemporary apostolic Christianity will be discovered in local churches only. The variety may be bewildering at first. We find apostolic Christianity in abandoned movie theaters, supermarket-modern chapels, moldering old steeple-topped clapboard relics, pseudo-Gothic cathedral-looking buildings, storefronts, and the Rockefeller-Riverside Church in New York City. But the spectacular variety is not really bewildering. It is most suitably apostolic. In fact, the rhetoric of ecumenism is bewildering. It is alarmed by this variety. It is forever calling "the church" to confess its variety as a Sin. But then ecumenism takes denominations seriously and has come to the conclusion that denominationalism has produced the disunity in the body of Christ. So it has set about the quixotic and apostolically frivolous task of healing the fissures in the body of Christ. What could be more bewildering than that?

A serious classification of contemporary apostolic Christianity in America pays no attention to denominations or to stylized theological descriptions of the local churches of a denomination. Such a classification goes straight to the localities in which these local churches exist. It focuses on kinds of localities because local churches invariably define themselves in local terms. A local people of God scarcely ever would hold on to a denominational affiliation as absolutely crucial. If pushed hard, it would eventually concede it could as well be Lutheran, without relinquishing everything. But it would never consider how it could be some *where* else, or that God would want it to be in another *no*-where. The *where* is the whole point, which a serious classification begins with.

In time it seems that the locality does a better job of converting the church than the church does in trying to convert the locality. The Congregational Church of Mill Valley, in Marin County, California, is more like Mill Valley than it is like the Reformed Church of Spring Valley, New York. It certainly does look as if Mill Valley converted the church.[2] For that matter, when we look at the church in Spring Valley, it is so much like Spring Valley that unless Spring Valley is called the church, investigation couldn't find any church at all. Sociologists are already tired of pointing that out, it has become so evident. The church mirrors social composition and class ranking. It fits into the locality, no matter what it is or where it is. But unsuspecting sociologists have not appreciated the irony of the situation inside the mind of the church—or the mind of Christ, which, the church says, amounts to the same thing.

In the mind of the church, it has played a prior role in forming the locality. Historians might treat that as a laughable bit of pride. But the church believes it is true. As I read Winthrop Hudson's *American Protestantism*,[3] the majority of local churches in the land west of the Eastern seaboard sprang up as a direct result of a drenching evangelical home-missionary enthusiasm. These zealous church-spreaders considered a locality without a church as not a real locality yet, and they did a total churching job on the vast Mississippi Valley first, then moved westward from that base.

Local churches are bonded to localities, even the "new church development" churches that began with three families in a suburban housing tract in 1950 and have now grown to 1,200 members. But they are more than just bonded. They have had a major hand in creating the localities in the first place. In the church's mind you couldn't write a decent history of Mill Valley without mentioning the role of the church. Without the church it probably would have sunk with the weight of its own paganism and boisterous sin into the bay. The same would be true of Spring Valley. It definitely is true of Chicago. The First Presbyterian Church there continues to point out at every one of its anniversaries how it was the very first church in Chicago, when Chicago was a stockaded *fort,* and how that valiant church's evangelical witness shaped Chicago from the very beginning.[4]

True, local churches seem to express more locality than divine origin, yet according to the vastly energetic founders of these churches, the locality was on the divine mind before a church was established there. They said it was the Gospel truth. The spectacle of culture swamping the church hides the prior spectacle of church swamping the culture, and so obscures the actual situation of church tediously swamping church.

Standard breakdowns of churches by reference to social class and economic and ethnic background are perfectly true. One would have to be blind and a fool not to acknowledge them instantly. There are churches for the rich and the poor, the Mexican and the Finn. And most all the churches hope, or once hoped, they could be like the churches for the rich. These conventional breakdowns show that the ranking of local churches (and the ranking of denominations) studiously copies and mirrors social composition with its classical ranks. This is true but not yet fully true. There has been a ranking for prior disposing at work that the conventional breakdowns miss. The social ranking did not grow up like weeds. It is the work of an earlier apostolic Christianity. The social composition so much alleged to have sullied the composition of the body of Christ *came* from the body of Christ. This fact may become clearer in an apostolically serious classification of contemporary local churches in America.

Successful Christianity Local Churches

We all know theological commentators have recently been emphasizing how low-down Christianity is. Transcultural, they call it. Christianity has no regard for one's social standing, one's pocketbook, one's skin color, or one's gender, they most recently add. They seem to be ashamed of the main kind of Christianity there is in America. It is successful Christianity. It can be found in successful local churches located in successful regions of the country. Chicago's North Shore, or Philadelphia's Mainline, or New York's Westchester County or Stamford, Connecticut. That they are suburban, exurban, urban, or rural is of no consequence. That they are where successful people live is the point.

The local churches in these localities are big and opulent. They display the success of the localities. Success, if not flauntable, is useless. Successful people of God flaunt their success discreetly. Good taste is next to godliness, they say. If we have a cathedral-looking church building, then let it be a species of Gothic architecture; if a modern-looking church building, then let I.M. Pei design it. It should look like a million dollars, either way. It does, too. It is like the homes of the successful people of God who go there.

The cornerstones of these successful Christianity local churches read, "To the Glory of God," and the buildings themselves will have memorial windows and elegant little plaques informing you that this room was paid for by some wealthy person or in memory of some wealthy person. It all amounts to the same thing. It was a glorious God who arranged for all this wealth.

Generally, people in successful localities attribute their success to free enterprise capitalism and to their good luck in being born American. The people of God in these places say much the same thing, but they add, significantly, that free enterprise capitalism and America were God's doing in the first place. God told them to live virtuous lives. Be thrifty, industrious, and sober, he said. These virtues are their own reward. He was right, too. They were. Christianity really pays.

Successful localities don't favor face-to-face community

even at parties, and definitely not in church. Success has nothing to do with face-to-face and its interpersonal burdens. Success is won by inspired individual effort, at times the effort of being born an heir. Sometimes successful people will admit the virtues of team play because in some endeavors it works better than individual performance. That would be the only reason. So the idea of a closely knit face-to-face community is not to be found in these localities, however much the New Testament favors it. The affections of Christ will be found in the church budget. And caring for the needs of the community will be assigned to well-paid assistant ministers. Both localities and their churches think of unknit communities that are large and important and composed of wealthy and important people. Communities are theaters for showing success.

So local churches in these localities do just that: They show success. They have fabulous budgets. They have lush endowments. They have rich worship services. Rich and important-looking ushers escort worshipers to their pews. They wear striped trousers and cutaway coats decorated with boutonnieres. The candelabra are golden, or at least sterling silver. The pipe organ cost $400,000. The preacher receives a salary of $30,000 a year. He imports his shoes from London. The quartet of soloists are professional musicians, and they are paid handsomely. The worshipers wear expensive clothes. The offering plates are lined with velvet. The rest rooms are clean. The furnace works. In summertime the air-conditioning system works, although most of the people of God are not around to enjoy it because they are away for the summer. The bulletins are printed each Friday afternoon in a no-nonsense Bodoni typeface. When the organist comes to the end of the special music and modulates tastefully through two keys to C Major, slowly pushes the great swell pedal, and begins the Doxology, the people of God know what it is all about. Praise God indeed from whom all blessings flow.

Successful Christianity local churches are supposed to attract the envious who will never be successful and the people who aspire to be successful and might make it. In that way the great ranks of pews provided in necessarily large "sanctuaries" have been filled. The actually successful pay for the church and do go to church whenever they are in town and feel like it. The envious and aspiring successful always go. These churches have real class, they say, not stopping to think that the majority of their fellow worshipers are retail clerks and dental technicians and not magnates at all.

But some of the traditional hordes of worshipers in these successful Christianity local churches are stopping to think, apparently, and aren't going to these churches any more in quite the same numbers. The success in the localities and expressed in the local churches has lately suffered from eroding doubts. Success once meant "more" or "faster" or "lots." It wasn't really decipherable because success was itself the cipher. Whatever it is, success is no longer held in quite the same universal envious regard it once enjoyed. We think of Morningside Heights, or Grosse Point, or Stamford, or Nob Hill as well-known successful localities now in some kind of trouble. They are typical of all successful localities and their local churches.

Successful people are no longer bathed in envy. They don't even envy each other. Certainly they no longer bother to give God the glory. If any glory is due, they say, give it to the tax specialist or the accountant. So the successful Christianity local churches are experiencing some malfunction, but not because they are short of money. They are short of worshipers.

Ironically, the last line of defense against the upsetting idea that privilege and power are not to be universally admired and envied has come to be a fresh assertion of the old

Gospel. The old Gospel says, "Christianity really pays." This is the driving heartbeat of all conservative-evangelical appeal. The best student of these complex matters, Richard Hofstadter, is now dead, so he can't comment on this latest manifestation of political-social conservatism defending the first and nineteenth centuries. But he taught us not to be surprised.

Community-Locality Local Churches

There is a testy sort of triumphalism among the great local churches, as though the truth of the central apostolic contentions rests on whether Christianity really does pay or not. These local churches are exceptional, as successful people are. For the most part, Americans are not successful. They are sometimes trying to be, but mostly they are not trying very hard. They have made compromises; they have had some bad luck. They are lazy. Yet while not aiming directly at really big success, they have achieved a modest but substantial comfort. So have the local churches in their localities.

These churches raise their chaste steeples, crosses, bell-towers to a sky they know to be beneficent. They are not prepossessing buildings. Their founding builders were not expecting a congregation of 2,000 someday. 200 would be about right. The church as a building lives the congregation. The modesty of the building expresses itself as a tranquility in the laissez faire congregation. And the modesty of the building in turn expresses the community-locality in which it exists as the center.

We have come to the waving grain, fruited plain, and purple mountains of this classification. The boundaries of a locality nicely match the glue of community solidarity. The local church is the center of the locality-community. Within the forethought of the local church founders, including the Divine Founder, the church would radiate its saving influence outward in all directions to the very ends of the community-locality. It would apply a subtle evangelical pressure on every facet of the community-locality's life. In time, the distinction between Christian and neighbor would become meaningless.

These community-localities understand themselves. This is an intimate, textured understanding. It is opaque to outsiders, who can't understand either the community or the locality. Under some unusual historical pressure they exhibit what they are to outsiders, who are generally surprised. One thinks of South Boston. When faced with a hated court order requiring a new racial composition in "their" schools, outsiders saw that there was no distinction between Christian and neighbor. Most every resident of the community and the locality reacted in the same way—disgusted resistance to the court order. Solidarity forever is the way of life in South Boston. The local churches there express the way of life. They are a part of it.

The direct experience of community, sometimes enduring through several generations, composes and reinforces the definition of the locality, which then injects a geographical exclusiveness into the everywhere-present experience of the community. And with frank apostolic certitude the local churches modestly express the *double* experience, of community and of locality. Else the incarnation doesn't mean much.

These people, so richly stitched into communities where everybody is alike, so comfortably bound with provincial definition, are the people of God in those places. They are good, Christ-like people. They are also and naturally pur-blind racists. They have to be. The idea of their community-locality is basically theological. God establishes churches to redeem peoples in neighborhoods. God knows his geography, and he knows his people too. He keeps his Anglos, Scots, Swedes, Finns, Lithuanians, Poles, Irish, Cubans, Puerto Ricans, blacks, Chinese, Japanese, Panamanians, and Italians in their own distinctive neighborhoods. The neighborhood may be three square blocks, half a block, or a small city of 25,000. It is the distinctive neighborhood that counts anyway, not its size. He intends to redeem each neighborhood. He does this by the generation, not by the week. Eventually there is no distinction between Christian and neighbor. That is how Christianity works.

In a typical community-locality of 2,500 there will be perhaps five local churches, each with an irrelevant denominational history. They are testimonies to a certain profligacy of divine initiative, no doubt, but as established congregations in discrete buildings, they live out apostolic Christianity. Before the community-locality, God was, and it came into existence at his hand and is sustained by his grace. Therefore in simply expressing the local way of life—itself Christ-like— each local church expresses a profoundly American grasp of divine providence. How else could apostolic Christianity be in America? Before one hastily concludes that these modestly radiant local churches have sold out the Gospel and the divine origin of *the* church, one must recollect that the Gospel and *the* church produced the community-localities in the first place. Some sell-out.

The Wrong Kind of Local Churches

For perfectly understandable theological reasons, there is authoritative racism and social condemnation in the United States. It is a theological fact more than it is a historical fact. The land is dotted with the socially condemned and the ethnic unmeltables. The suspicion of economic oppression rises regularly among them. At any rate, in the land of comfort and plenty, lots of people are not comfortable. They tend to live in localities too, just like regular Americans, and these localities are variously called ghettos, Mexican town, the wrong side of the tracks, and so on. There is very little experience of community in these localities. It looks as though these people are huddled together, but they aren't. They are huddled against each other in ongoing fear and loathing. They have come to understand that the general American has said, You are rotten people. They believe this is a statement of fact.

Therefore, when local churches arise in these localities, they are as marginal as life in the localities is. Abandoned theaters are typical local church buildings in these localities, or abandoned regular local churches. In big cities storefronts are typical. The buildings are falling apart, as the localities are. But the congregations are cells of warm contentment. They have no tradition, and cannot trace themselves backward at all. They come straight over 2,000 years from the mind of God. They have instant and total understanding of Pentecost because in their theological life it happened yesterday. And it must be quickly noted that this understanding does not come directly from local church or from preaching. To suppose that too quickly ignores the primary voice of the locality.

The place in which social condemnation is shovelled together will not be able to provide much coherent explanation, since the place itself is an absolute incoherence. There is no sense to a ghetto. It is an historical absurdity. There is no history here other than mini-intraghetto history, which explains the internal shape of social misery but not how the misery is related to Alexander the Great or Jonathan Edwards. The eloquence of the locality is remarkable. The locality says there is no history anyway. And then so does the local church.

Pentecost is totally and instantly understood. It *is* the Bible of these local churches. Moses and those other people back there have almost no interest. In the hands of black power zealots, we all know, Moses was regularly presented as a black deliverer, a prototype of Jesus, who was the black Messiah. But among the Wrong Kind of Local Churches, Moses' experience is considered a species of Pentecost. He came out, you see. He passed over. He fell into the hands of the Mighty Spirit, trembled, shuddered, shook, and became in surrender the Spirit's tool. The other people back there have interest if, like Moses, they had interesting kinds of ecstatic experience.

The main thing is that God broke out at Pentecost as a mighty spiritual power and promised to be with his church as that power. He keeps his promises every Sunday, morning, afternoon, and evening; also on Wednesday and Friday nights, and in some churches on every night of the week. The people gather. They sing. They pray. They read from the Bible. One of the brothers or sisters then preaches and, as promised, out of the preaching comes a restlessness, an anticipation; and as the preaching comes stronger, the anticipated fulfillment of the divine promise begins to happen. The Spirit comes! The people submit to its coming. They begin to shout and dance. Some of them begin speaking in tongues—strange languages of the Spirit that sound exactly like childish or psychotic babble to outsiders. The people become frenzied in the power of the Spirit. They get caught up in ecstacy, until there is something like a moment of climax. After that the power of the Spirit begins slowly to subside. Still moist with spiritual exertion, and feeling wonderful, these people of God go home and to bed.

The people of God know in truth who they are in those moments of ecstacy and belief. They know so much and they love God so much that were they to die right then, that would be fine. In fact, the future is wiped out no less than the past. And before official theologians reckon with this obliteration, the voice of the locality must first be heard.

It says insistently that there is no future. The idea of potential futures is laughable because they will all be some cruel and disappointing joke. That is the concrete expectation. It comes from realism. There is a future all right, which the locality does recognize, and in the moment of recognition turns away from. "There is no future" means "there is no future worth thinking about." And when the local churches in these localities want to die on the spot and go straight to heaven, the locality is saying its piece.

These local churches are authentic apostolic Christianity. They are in a place as the people of God there. And while there is a species of sociological analysis that can identify something like a core of resentment among those people of God, the analysis aborts at the critical point. The analysis assumes that these people replace a hideous future in the real world with a glorious future in heaven, the fabled pie in the sky. Well, was it ever *resentment?* Are these people of God specifically angry about the social abuse they suffer? The voice of the locality does not say resentment. It says resignation. It does not say, Stand up and fight! Bestir yourselves! Move on the Man! It says the opposite: that resentment is the pie in the sky, a luxury no better afforded than a new home in Stamford. These people of God are already next door to heaven, in precisely the same way they are practically in Pentecost. It is pie *in the church* all the time.

The other people of God in other localities have had an actual hand in obliterating the history and the future of these localities of social condemnation. These acts are historical; they are the work of apostolic Christianity. In a torrent of profound incoherence, the people of God in the condemned sector express the very same richly authenticated reality by

drawing Pentecost and heaven within the perimeter of contemporary direct experience. They have an assignation with
the Spirit. Tonight! They are going to church. They can't
wait. There is no resentment in that local church. Ain't no
flies on Jesus, either.

There are drive-in churches, TV churches, cathedrals pars-
ing the hours with cloistering Westminster changes, little
churches trying to be big churches, superdenominational
local churches, big churches growing backward into little
churches, abandoned churches, museum churches where
tourists enter to stare, local churches that begin one way and
transmute to something else, local churches masterminded
by shyster preachers who get rich, house churches, local
churches without buildings at all. Each one of them could be
classified according to its own local eccentricity. That is the
secret of an apostolic classification. You go straight to the
local eccentricity. Apostolic Christianity assigns itself local
careers; it is its local topography.

Localities have histories, even the ones with a no-history.
The history of a locality is not, however, merely past. It endures powerfully. "The past is not even past."[5] Once there
was no locality. Then it was founded. The founding began
expressing itself in the acts of social institution, which institutions began expressing themselves, still do, and will throughout the existence of the locality. Once there was no church
building. Then Christians decided to build one. Their decision is concretized in the building they put up, and it lives
on through the building. If they furnished it with a splendid
four-manual pipe organ, their decision will endure. It will
shape the character of worship, the type of music played,
likely the type of liturgy used, the musical program of church
and community, the temperature in the biggest room of the
whole building, hence every budget that people of God ever

draws up. A building without Sunday school rooms speaks loudly all the time about a disdain for church education.

Localities with textured traditions of community observance impress themselves powerfully on their local churches. Custom, typical behavior, common understanding are not preserved as psychical objects or mere memories; they endure in the locality as its properties. Predecessors are powerful presences; they are willful. Traditions began sometime, and they endure because of how they started. They, too, are willful. They are, exactly, *meta*topographical. Local churches develop and change, but within the limits assigned by metatopographical factors. The powerful determination of predecessors, of traditions, of common self-understanding, if violated, produces a crisis in identification; if it is successfully violated, the emerging local church will have a *new* identity, expressive of its new founding, and then *it* will begin to determine and shape the future existence of that local church.

A church is supposed to do something in some *there*. Unless we assume a completely ineffectual and useless churchly presence in the locality, the church will be or do something like it was intended to be or do in the certified location. That is the way apostolic Christianity gets into topography as an added, metatopographical presence. It is designed that way. It is not social determinism, it is apostolic Christianity meeting itself when it meets and is lived by the past. It does what it says. It works.

The Nation Could Sue!

Churches in Amarillo, Texas, and Bangor, Maine, are not alike. The Holy Trinity Episcopal Church is not like the Powerhouse Church of God in Christ in the U.S.A., Inc., either. La Ecclesia de Jesus Christo is not like a Missouri Synod

Church of the Redeemer. They are all different. But they are all sensationally local. Local churches are all we can see, everywhere we look. How else could they all be so regularly local? Why is there so little critical distance between a local church and its locality? What is it that abolishes so regularly the very distinction between church and locality? We have to begin believing there is a metalocal pressure subtly, perhaps spectrally, at work here.

Historians of American ideas would find such a possibility agreeable. In fact, Perry Miller's best known essay describes the self-conscious super-Christianity of the Puritans and how they conceived of their voyage to a new land as an "errand into the wilderness."[6] This premiere historian of American ideas mischievously concludes that they were bushwhacked *by* the wilderness, or by some spectral proto-American force.

Something happened when Christianity first stepped ashore in America. And it has kept on happening. At the very beginning the experience of being here in America began defining the *here*. The first Christians here were destiny's darlings. They thought of themselves that way. They were entering a promised land, they already knew. They developed an appropriate theology for themselves. It was appropriately American. And it has endured with a stubborn willfulness in the "American mind" ever since. It is, in fact, the very metalocal pressure producing all these local churches.

The Christianity that stepped ashore was orthodox Calvinism. It didn't remain orthodox very long. Perry Miller is spellbound by the modifications that occurred because they were so outrageously American. In observing the procedure of modification, he thinks he has found the grand event in American intellectual history.[7] It is worth our attention too.

The Puritan pastor-theologians who came to northeastern America and called it New England shortly began to develop some new thoughts. Orthodox Calvinism is a pretty strenuous business. For one thing it demands belief in God's implacable righteousness and in God's plenary forgiveness. These concepts do not rest easily together. Calvin tied them together with the bailing wire of Majesty. A Majestic God can do whatever occurs to such a Being to do, including the choice to speak in the Holy Bible. The first American theological thinkers, orthodox Calvinists to the core, began right there at that leading Calvinist doctrine. They began to lower some of the Calvinist tension, let off some Calvinist steam. The Puritan divines wanted something a little closer to what they knew about God in their thriving holy laboratory called New Israel.

What they did was replace the idea of illimitable Majesty with the idea of a covenant of grace. That just this idea occurred to them is more than merely remarkable, or fortuitous, or scriptural. There is really no accounting for it, unless, of course, one wants to entertain the thesis of some spectral "wilderness" pressure.

These enterprising Americanizers understood a covenant to be a contract, a legal arrangement, a bargain struck by covenanting partners. A covenant has terms the contracting parties agree on, what the partners promise to do. The promises are binding. While this understanding of a covenant is more commercial than it is biblical, the Puritan divines used it to reorganize biblical history. For them the big Bible events occurred when God and Adam covenanted (Genesis 2), when God and Abraham covenanted (Genesis 17), and when God and the Christian Church covenanted (after Christ). The Puritan divines thought God enters into direct contractual relationships with human beings and said the Bible says so.

The covenant with Adam consisted of two parts. Adam contracted to keep God's moral law, the understanding of which God had placed in his heart. God contracted to provide Adam with eternal life. This was the covenant of works. Adam did not live by his covenanted agreements. He was therefore damned on the spot; since he was the "federal" representative of all human beings, they, too, were damned.

Not content with such a quick sinful outcome in his human creation, God decided to institute a new covenant. He called it the covenant of grace. This is the one we read about in Genesis 17. As the Puritan divines read the scripture, they found the covenant of grace had two parts also. God entered into this covenant with Abraham. God promised to send Christ the Mediator and would count faith in this promise as the activity required for the granting of salvation and felicity. On his part Abraham had to promise to be "perfect," "upright," and "without hypocrisy."

The covenant of grace matured with the coming of Christ the Mediator. Under its terms God promises salvation and felicity (new life) to those who believe Christ *is* the Mediator. That is his part. The Christian church, and hence its members, individual Christians, promises to believe Christ is the Mediator and to live godly lives without hypocrisy. If they fail in their efforts to keep their promise, since this is a covenant of grace not works, they may plead for forgiveness.

The spectacular result of this theological work is that the mighty illimitable sovereign of the universe has now chained himself into a fairly sensible, just, and reasonable program of action. While God is no doubt capable of radical divine action any time, the elect covenanted believers have a good deal more assurance of predictable grace than Calvin provided them with. And by attesting to the articles of the covenant in the present time, altered, of course, by the coming of the Mediator, the ancient divine promises are automatically and legally binding. The believer can *sue* for the benefits of the covenant.

When in later generations the idea of covenant assumes

concrete political shape in the founding of the republic, it carries an invisible and transcendental baggage. Even the *idea* is divinely guaranteed. Were God to fail in the divine part of the bargain, the *nation* could sue![8]

When these Reverend Thinkers stepped ashore onto America, they believed that the issue of election and damnation was settled. God had settled it before he created the world. They were orthodox Calvinists. They believed in double predestination. Without quite giving up the belief that some are elected to grace and some to damnation, they Americanized it. Whatever God may have predisposed, it looked to them as if the human beings involved had the choice to affirm or reject the predisposed election. In fact, it looked as if anyone who affirmed the proposition that Christ is the Mediator had driven a good hard bargain with God.

Suddenly the trancendental drama of election and rejection has been transposed from the councils of heaven to the very local meetinghouse, where the preaching of the covenant confronts sinful human beings with a divine "suitor." The matter of entering into the covenant has become a decision for human beings to make—an idea repulsive to Calvinism and yet the cornerstone of revivalist theology that would blossom later across the continent. Naturally, the Puritan thinkers hedged on the drama in the meetinghouse with orthodox reminders of the prior drama played out in the councils of heaven, maintaining that whatever happens was predestined to happen anyway. But it was maintained almost as a throwaway line. Practically, eternal salvation (with annexed earthly felicity) and eternal perdition came to issue in church. Here is where the procedures of localization were born. The meetinghouse is not an incidental place. It is the *very* place where the most important decisions in the universe are made each Sabbath. In the meetinghouse Christianity gets utterly local.

In similar fashion the Puritan divines reconstituted faith and grace more in line with their experience; then they hammered out an idea that would later become notoriously American: The preaching of the covenant has a moral authority for the unbeliever no less than for the believer. Believers are naturally in a happier position. On hearing strictly moral requirements, they must earnestly try to obey. That is their part of the bargain. If they fail, they can flee to Christ for forgiveness. That is God's part of the bargain. Unbelievers also must try to obey the preached requirements, which are good and just in themselves. But failing, unbelievers have no Christ to flee to, hence no forgiveness. That they even hear what is required is a species of grace in itself. They have a *chance* to believe, after all. But believing or not, as they choose, unbelievers must perform what is morally required, or else they re-earn a richly merited eternal perdition.

Thereby the meetinghouse came to be understood as the scene of a further drama. The affairs of business, social arrangement, and civil government were brought to the attention of the entire neighborhood with clearly instituted ecclesiastical force. The church says the New Testament says the apostles say God says, *No work on the sabbath,* for example. In fact, the drama in the meetinghouse accounts for the definition of a neighborhood—a parish, no less. In the parish-neighborhood-locality God gets the worldly business done, through the church in its living middle. In the meetinghouse its affairs and its destiny are authoritatively brought to moral light.

Perry Miller finds these developments intellectually explicable but nonetheless astonishing. His humorous asides provide a running testament of his unbelief that human beings could actually *think* these things without laughing—an enterprise at which he, at any rate, regularly fails. But taking either the uncut or the modified Calvinism as a norm, the other has been destroyed more than merely compromised.

More emerges from this early covenant theology than has ever been disclaimed, either by Jonathan Edwards a generation later, or by every other later Calvinist in American theological history. It would be simply wrong to argue that these *very* formulations have had a traceable historical career. But it would be equally wrong to ignore the extent to which versions of and differently formulated ideas of similar substance have "somehow" found their way into local church Christianity. They do have an exemplary importance, yet their connection with what continues to emerge to this day is described as another of those discontinuities, or, as Perry Miller would say, is *best* left alone.

It seems that every sort of apostolic Christianity that came to America eventually became American Calvinism, whether Free Will Methodists, Quakers, or Roman Catholics. It probably was in the wilderness—that "spectral" thesis again. However that may have been, it certainly got into and may still be found all over the country in the shape of very local apostolic Christianity. The church is the house of the people of the covenant; the church is the theological principle for defining a neighborhood. These are contemporary ideas. That God is bound by his Word to save and to bless can also be found, as virtually the entire apparatus of civil religion. Because of this covenanting core, the people of the United States have been blessed with a civil government that enjoys a rich scriptural warrant and protracted divine care— a thesis grown dog-eared through recent bicentennial discourse, and probably untrue, as Hannah Arendt suggests.[9] It was a rare intellectual achievement to have thought that local church Christianity is the only kind there is. But by its overwhelming success and continued restatement, it now exists as a crashing banality.

In this theological development the dominant and probably most important legacy has been the routinization and domestication of election-providence. This is the specific American component of American Calvinism. As a feature of civil religion, it assumes that God works through a system of secondary causes in history and in nature to bless the nation, New Israel, which has at its center the elect, New Israel. The Puritan divines were fond of the idea that God does not ordinarily resort to miracle, in which the series of primary causes is disrupted; he can creatively and cunningly manipulate the system of secondary causes to perform miracles that for all the world look like ordinary historical life. There is, therefore, no need for theologians to point with specificity to the particular places and circumstances of God's providential activity, since the activity is assumed to be occurring behind the very structure of all occurrence. American Calvinism assumes it always is.

Individual Christian Americans have come to believe God works toward their personal welfare full time in the same way he works for the nation's and the church's welfare. They have gone the covenant theology one better. Christianity is a very personal religion, and God has outrageously personal relations with individual Christians. The extreme limit of localization has been reached when the individual, the absolutely local, is a self-conscious reason for there being Christianity at all. And this is the case with individual Christian American belief. This is not mysticism or existentialism. This is a specific kind of American Calvinism. It is Yahoo Calvinism. It arose in local church Christianity as the *most local of all*. And it is widespread.

Official theologians express ritual dismay at Yahoo Calvinism, as well they might.[10] But they have no grounds for surprise. The discontinuity between Yahoo Calvinism and cove-

nant theology is no greater than the discontinuity between
covenant theology and regular Pauline-Augustinian Calvinism. In America Yahoo Calvinism is the most authentic Christianity there is because it is the *most* local and is at least as
Christian as any other kind. Yahoo Calvinism comes down to
a specifically vain and tendentious centering of the local
church in the neighborhood as the explicating wing of provi-
dence-election to the inevitably individual Christian, who
then knows God will provide.

When confronted with these present realities in our active
contemporary experience—"living still" before our eyes—
we begin to perceive dimly the immensity of the blunder
that thought to substitute a divine origin for the historical
origin of the church. From the distance afforded by looking
at 300 years of American church history within its natural
continuum of 2,000 years of *church* history, the blunder appears in its enormous proportions.

The most provincial expressions of a largely comic chau-
vinism seem to be proceeding from sure Christian consciousness. The Puritan divines were certain apostolic legatees.
They *knew* what God says, they said. Jonathan Edwards'
heroic attempts to restore some Calvinist balance were instantly traduced by his enthusiastic brother preachers and by
the assemblies of local church Christians and proto-Chris-
tians who listened, most of whom did not care *either way*.
When the norms have themselves been localized, and ecclesiastical authority is automatically populist, it makes no
Christian sense to appeal to the extralocal norm of bloody old
John Calvin, for instance.

There it is: peculiarly fated, disposed, ordained by the very
internal self-understanding of American apostolic Christianity, guaranteed by a divinely clad historical procession of
ecclesiastical authority and by a tradition that can metamor-
phose in any direction it chooses and claim any authority it

wants. It can be deflected from its course, if at all, by preaching, which, naturally, it authorizes.

And there are no brakes on the Great Apostolic Blunder Machine.

4. Worship, or Here Comes the Collection Plate

Local churches worship God. Worship is not just the "religious side," something done in order to add balance to bowling, softball, hayrides, square dances, marathon seminars, and potluck suppers—the fabled "social side." Worship is local church Christianity's main activity. In worship the past of church tradition meets the divinely illuminated future. Although the cognitive claims seem a little thin, worshiping congregations maintain that God is present with them when they worship. Didn't Jesus promise as much?

I follow here the last-ditch effort of American denominational Protestantism to reassert itself as something new, that is, as a fully ecumenical Protestant church, something called *COCU* (Council of Churches Uniting). The COCU "Plan of Union"[1] describes worship this way (Fasten your seat belts):

Christian worship is the response of celebration and thanksgiving for God's holy love revealed in Jesus Christ. It is mixed with joy and praise in his presence, with sorrow and repentance for our sins and failures, with petitions for the needs of others and of ourselves, and with hope in God's renewing grace and strength.

Through our awe-filled recognition of the indescribable wonder and reality of God, we are enabled to join with those who, in all times and places, have offered the sacrifice of praise and obedience to "Christ Jesus, who died, yes, who was raised from the dead, who is at the right hand of God, who indeed intercedes for us" (Romans 8:34). We are able to make this response because Jesus our Lord has made it perfectly in our own human nature. He joins us to himself in this response by the renewing power of the Holy Spirit, whom he has sent to us from his Father to abide with us forever. (VI.1)

This is a high-blown statement that local church Christians wouldn't put that way but would agree with. The main Christian hour of the week is Sunday between 11 A.M. and noon. Churchly custom has chosen this hour as the worship hour. Christian attendance at worship expresses loyalty to the church. God counts loyalty to *his* church, after all, as loyalty to God. However that may be, attending worship is the distinctive thing Christians do. They gather together. They sing hymns, pray, listen to scripture, listen to preaching, listen to the announcements, listen to the special music, share the Lord's Supper, and baptize new Christians.

A Big Business Supported by Local Church Cash

The crucial activity of worship for God probably is the singing of the Gloria. It goes, "Glory be to the Father, and to the Son, and to the Holy Ghost." This pleases him. But church leaders find the crucial activity in another part of the worship service. What they find crucial they are never blunt about, however. See if you can find it in this statement made by the COCU "Plan of Union":

The church as a community of believers requires the best of their skills and attention. A united church is needed to conserve and develop the gains being made by Christians who put their primary effort into the mission in the world. Responsibility for the institution is a shared task, but the laity must lead in the under-girding of the mission of the church through conscientious stewardship of time, talents, and possessions. Their responsibility in the church includes full participation in the government of the church, the establishment of policy, and the articulations of standards. (VII.24)

Unless you are a lifelong observer of church leaders, you probably missed it. It is "conscientious stewardship of time, talents, and possessions." That is an artful way of saying *Cash*. It must be artfully said because church leaders don't want to be thought commercial. But it must be said somehow because they regard the offering as the crucial activity in worship. Without the offering, poof! No more Christianity, they say.

There is a realism here, all right. All of this Christianity costs money. Christians know that. If they have any doubts, church leaders explain the facts to them. This very church building they are giving the offering in costs money to operate, for instance, as it cost money to build. The staff of the church can't do God's work full-time for nothing. Employees (the church leaders plus helping staff) must be paid. Outside this local church there are thousands of selfless Christian people engaged in Christ's Mission who also need to be paid. Add to that the seminaries in need. Professors there make scarcely $18,000 a year. How selfless can Christians get? On top of that, there are Christian hospitals, schools, orphanages, colleges, institutes, clinics, and academies. It is all God's work. God gave his only Son for us, Christians say. The least we can do is give money for his work.

The gifts to the church to do God's work may be a casual 85 cents a week or a hefty $50 a month. As church leaders everywhere insist, it is not the size of the gifts that counts, or even the spirit in which they are given, but their regularity.

"Every week" is the part church leaders emphasize. Without consistency in giving, the entire superstructure of local church Christianity would fall into ruin.

There are sporadic special fund-raising drives. Local churches on their own raise money at bazarrs, bake sales, festivals, banquets, and rummage sales. But this is insignificant social cash. The big ongoing cash on which local church Christianity depends comes in when the offering plate is passed each week.

The major denominations are each embarked on special fund-raising campaigns. The United Presbyterians, the United Methodists, and the Protestant Episcopalians are going after $60 million, $80 million, or $100 million, and so on.[2] The campaigns will last four to six years. In the same period local church Christians in these same denominations will give between $4.8 and $8.4 *billion* in the offering plate —at a rate of $1.6 billion a year.[3]

This is how it works: out of the corner of the eye, nothing direct. Local church Christians "somehow" find themselves at the providential center of things. In worship they see the flags and hear the drums of a triumphal kingdom of God. They see the forces of righteousness advancing on the forces of paganism. The outcome is never in doubt. God will prevail —provided his church has enough money to do the job.

The Christian success story is tirelessly told. It is the church's favorite story. First there were twelve apostles at Pentecost. Before the first day in the church's life was over, there were thousands of Christians. From that good beginning in Jerusalem, the church, enduring martyrdom along the way, eventually triumphed over the whole Roman Empire and became the Empire itself. Think of it! In a mere 300 years or so.

First a struggling band of Pilgrims who fled to America because they loved God, and now a Christian America with millions of Christians giving their money to pay for a mission drive that can't be satisfied until there is a Christian world. What a Christianity! It really does work.

It is Christianity's inevitable expansion that recommends itself out of the corner of the eye in worship. It mustn't be direct, church leaders know. It must be said quickly and obliquely. God will be disappointed if that cash doesn't keep rolling in. If it were said too directly, then a major doubt might be encouraged. Christians might well think that a Mighty God wouldn't be without other resources to accomplish his will. So it is said another way in order to keep the spotlight of motivation on God's none-too-obvious decision to accomplish his ends through the means of local church Christianity.

There is a needy world out there, local church Christians are told. *And,* the unvoiced pitch goes, God has decided to meet these needs through you Christians right here in this church. The targets range from starvation to pagan unbelief. Doubtless a generous humane concern for starving and for pagan people animates Christian givers. It is a concern authorized by apostolic preaching and example. But no matter how humane, the giving is related more fundamentally to the spread of Christianity. The Christian gives cash to support God's will. God uses the cash to make a witness. The witness works. Fresh Christians are added to the church, who give their cash to support God's will, which makes further witness, producing yet more fresh Christians, more cash, and so on. The spectacle of feeding the hungry is bound to make an impression on the world. The church is really on the ball, the world is supposed to say. The church really does love people.

A humane concern for starving people doubtless animates the thousands of church leaders above the local church level too. They are the price local church Christianity must pay for being successful. Their salaries and upkeep come off the top of any cash local church Christians give to Christ's Mission. As these church leaders see the matter, it is at least as important to keep the church going as it is to feed the immediately starving. Flashing a brilliant smile, these church leaders remind local church Christians that if the church is insufficiently staffed and funded now, the starving of tomorrow will not be fed. Where could they look for Christian generosity if there were no big church to administer the feeding programs?[4]

There is a big church as well as the local churches. In fact, investigation concludes that official apostolic Christianity in America is a big business supported by local church cash. It does not look at itself that way, of course. It doesn't even look at itself in denominational terms any more. It is a series of "levels" *added to* the grass roots, or local church, level. Christianity is a homogenious reality that has these levels, church leaders say. It is all local church Christianity, because all the levels beyond the local church serve it and help it be what it is. Naturally, the support levels are the first thing God intends local churches to support, for without them the local churches couldn't do their job of supporting God.

In the COCU "Plan of Union" we find first a district coordinating level just above the local level. It enables the local level to enter into cooperative endeavors. Next, there is a regional level, designed to coordinate districts and provide planning assistance to district level Christianity. Finally, there is a national level; it coordinates regional level activities and provides overall program and policy direction not only to the regional but to district and local levels, too. Each level is a distinctive and authentic piece of the same Christianity.

Homogeneity is what the level theory aims for. It is composed for local church Christian givers, who, looking at the

whole enterprise, will see one single reality, called Christ's
Mission. There is a self-sacrificing missionary in Korea, an
accountant in New York City, a regional executive in Cleveland, a doctor in New Mexico, a teacher in Chicago, a systems
expert, a seminary, a college, a radio program, a computer,
a World Council of Churches meeting in Nairobi, an emer-
gency airplane trip to Oklahoma City, office rent, a school in
Honduras, secretaries, printing costs, pension plans for
preachers, educational experts—and it is *all* Christ's Mission.
It all coheres; it all must be paid for. The level theory accom-
plishes a modern miracle after the manner of its Lord. Five
missionaries and four doctors are used to feed five thousand
. . . bureaucrats.

Concern for Numbers Is Built In

How tempting the complexity of this big church big business is to investigation! There is so much material here that
merely describing it would make Sören Kierkegaard's *Attack
upon Christendom* seem like a guerrilla raid. How seduc-
tively it all beckons! The paradoxes, the amazing antinomies,
the labrynthine connections present themselves eagerly.
How level theory replaced denominational theory.[5] How
denominational theory got that way. American history would
have to be considered. The traditions would have to be as-
sessed. We would have to get into angry arguments with
disputing scholars. And the National Council of Churches
would have to be analyzed, at the least. As a consequence,
investigation would be lost in institutional space forever, beguiled by complexity away from its primary task.

Interesting as these subjects are, they are not our fundamental concern. We are interested to discover the problem
local church Christianity has become to itself. We are dedi-
cated, remember, to the simple. We want to stick to the facts.

The facts are that local church Christianity isn't working, according to its own treasured understanding of itself. Local church Christianity has not read this dirty suspicion in the newspapers; it arises within local church Christianity as a suspicion about itself. The facts are also that local church Christianity is dangerously near idolatry when it says God has chosen it *exclusively* to get the divine job done in the world. According to its own scriptures the Christian church has plenty of reason to be worried about idolatry. The God of scriptures did, of course, ordain the church to be his missionary agent in the world. No doubt about that. But the same God of those same scriptures still has some decency about him and might reject the church if it were to faithlessly pursue its own ends instead of his. In that the possibility of idolatry arises. It never occurs to local church Christianity that God might reject it for unfaithfulness. What does occur to it is that if there is any unfaithfulness to be noted, it would more likely be God's than the church's.

There is a widespread anxiety in this local church Christianity about just how effective God really is. This is a historical anxiety, and it is as unstoppable as the very history producing the anxiety. This is not an anxiety produced by moral consideration: that what God is said to be doing and who God is said to be is unjust. Such considerations do arise. They have been isolated from this consideration of the church proper. Investigation has placed them in the zone of theology, and they will be dealt with in Part III. In the zone of the church proper, anxiety pops up because local churches are not growing. Christianity is not spreading from here to there. There isn't enough cash, or as much as there used to be. The future that revelation is supposed to illuminate on Sunday mornings doesn't feature the invincibly advancing kingdom of God. Its flags are limp and the drum beat erratic.

Here are these glorious church buildings whose founders

set pews to accommodate 900 worshipers. Now 35 come on Sunday mornings and 200 on Easter—at the most, on *good* Easters. Here are these Sunday school rooms for all ages, almost empty. Six children here, four children there. No youth class at all. What is wrong? the members ask church leaders. They tell the members to study their church sociology. Your natural membership has moved away and died. Both. You are not set up to attract new members. You've got to attract new members.

So the members of the local church go to workshops in order to learn church sociology. They are desperate. They must grow, they realize. They must make a comeback. They will find a way to be interesting to new members. The church sociology they learn is otherwise called evangelism. It says nothing about class or social ranking. It doesn't mention hard hats, the Protestant elite, ethnic unmeltables, ennui, or anything remotely like that. Church sociology is not sociology with church interest tacked on. Church sociology is called *Evangelism.* It is cutting out all the monkey business and talking about Jesus Christ, but in such a way that Jesus Christ will be interesting. People do not want to hear about what a dreary place the modern world is, and how full of problems, and how Jesus Christ is for peace or justice or against police brutality. Absolutely not. People want to hear about Jesus Christ's abilities to save, and his great way with unhappiness. Tell people that and they will be interested.

In time the local church works up a campaign to win new members to the church, at the same time making a smashing attack on unhappiness. Actually, there is little difference between the new campaign and what has always been done. But it seems new and promising and is something to do. It can't hurt, these local church Christians say. But it doesn't work. The potential new members don't find Jesus Christ interesting, even when he is talked about in an interesting way. Those who do are already going to some other, *wrong,* kind of local church. The others just aren't interested in Jesus Christ one way or another.

Something has gone bad, obviously. These local church Christians love their church. They believe it is a good church. They believe it should grow. They believe this is a divine promise, because the church's founding was God's doing. Yet the church is dying, not growing. The longer it goes, the deader it gets. When stripped of its divine guarantee of growth and new life, church members can read the grim facts plainly enough. In another ten years or so, maybe sooner, they will have to sell.

That is the problem local church Christianity is in. It is dying. It is losing out to paganism, to sin, to unrighteousness, to the secular spirit, to the modern world: all those areas where its own understanding of itself provides maximum assurance that it will always win. And all it knows is how to be itself. Has God forgotten his promises? Have local churches misunderstood God? That couldn't be true. So it must be something else. It must be bad technique. And they try harder. They study church sociology some more. And they continue to die.

They are not all dying at the same rate. Here, for instance, is a local church that fifteen years ago was a dynamic center for the liberal-to-radical politics of a small city. Its pews were always full then. It had an energetic relevant Bible preacher. Its membership was over 1,000, and many were active in the church's diverse programs. They came to church, too. They gave their money. The church, in turn, gave its money to worthy causes. But now the fortunes of the church have turned.

Its membership is edging downward. Everything it has always done it is now doing. Its music is as tasteful as ever. True, the new preacher is not as interesting as others the

church has had, but he is engaging and at least as good as any
other preacher in the city. The Christian education program
is well conceived and well run. There are interesting things
for church members to do on the "social side." But the desolating fact is that this church is dying. It will not die in ten
years, or twenty, but likely in twenty years it will have thirty-
five people showing up on Sunday mornings and will be
where so many other terminal local churches are right now
—feverishly studying church sociology. It doesn't want to
think about that, for sure. It wants to think it can reverse the
downward trend and make a comeback. But when it does
think hard about its future—without the divine guarantee—
it knows it, too, will die, just like the others. Its problem is
that it can't think of itself without the divine guarantee.

Were local church Christianity to think of itself in historical terms, then it could understand that like the Grange, the
D.A.R., the Mom 'n' Pop grocery store, the small liberal arts
college, the local church is a social institution that no longer
plays a necessary role in the life of the society. Society develops new institutions. Society needs professional football more
than it needs local churches. It needs television. It needs
sensitivity marathons. It needs one of those great unworldly
Eastern religions and not the local church. The local church,
like all outworn institutions, does not instantly die, anymore
than old soldiers; it withers away. It will be rugged all right.
It will resist death. But eventually it dies. As Chatauqua died.
As vaudeville died. As carriage making died. They were no
longer useful. Something better came along; something
more useful.

But this is precisely what local church Christianity cannot
do. It cannot look at itself as a social institution with a merely
historical career, following a merely historical founding. It
must consider its divine origin. It has to take account of

Pentecost. It must rehearse for itself all over again the cardinal understanding that:

☐ THE NEW TESTAMENT SAYS THE APOS-
TLES SAY GOD SAYS THE CHURCH IS THE
BODY OF CHRIST.

It must then be anxious and disappointed because history seems to have gotten the upper hand over God.

There is no gauche concern for mere numbers in these desolating recognitions. The people of God know better than to measure Christian success with numbers alone. It is certainly true that a small(er) congregation can pray together, stay together, and enjoy Christ's love quite as well as a big, growing congregation. If only there weren't that constant pressure built into the small(er) congregation. Its very reason for existence is to grow bigger, to spread the enjoyment of Christ's love to the very ends of the world, as its scriptures suggest. One could say a gauche concern for numbers was built into the very origin of the church. It was put there by the apostles or by God. Numbers have always been the way the Christian success story has been told.

Pentecost, then the Roman Empire. The pilgrims, then a Christian America. A Christian America, soon a Christian world. How can local church Christianity simply give up numbers as the basic way to understand itself?

There is cold comfort in the fact that not all local church Christianity is plagued with the problem of its dying. The Wrong Kind of local churches are not all dying. That's for sure. Some of them only feel like the Wrong Kind. They are actually the *Right* Kind. You can tell because they have so much money, which the Wrong Kind, by definition, never have. They are growing at a terrific clip. They have cut out all the monkey business altogether. They talk about Jesus

Christ only. They use New Testament language only. They act like Pentecost was last week. They lack neither members nor cash. They have plenty of both. And they have belief to spare. They believe anything, the more unbelievable the better, apparently.

We look at them on television. They have the money to buy good—often prime—time. They tell the old, old story, except they don't even have to tell it. They name it. They quote tiny pieces of the Bible. Christ died for you. You are a sinner. Believe and you will be saved from everlasting damnation. Only believe. That's all. Just like ... *TV itself.* Just send in your name, we'll do the rest. We'll rush you the new records, books, magazines, handsome photographs. You can send cash or we'll bill you. Or you can use your Master Charge.

It's so simple. We look at (Dr.) Jerry Falwell on television. He is building a Christian college in Virginia, it seems. He wants to furnish Christian young people with a real Christian education, without any of this modern stuff. The college will cost several million dollars. And he'll never go in debt, he promises. He'll build as the Christian dollars come in. Christ died for you—*free of charge*—so send those dollars in. Here is our address, (Dr.) Jerry Falwell says, the place you can send your dollars to.

Here is the 700 Club having a television marathon, just like muscular dystrophy. It gets $1 million in seventy-two hours, just like muscular dystrophy (which gets $26 million). What does the 700 Club need a million dollars for? Why, to carry on its television ministry. What is its television ministry? Why, saving souls, of course.

Here is (Dr.) Bill Bright and his Campus Crusade organization taking out the best prime time on a major network in order to wind up his national "I Found It" campaign. What has he found? That in only believing you get a bonus. It is

happiness. You get transformed. That's what you *find*. There
you were, a dreary piece of modern life, stewing around in
aimless ennui, trying booze, money, pot, divorce, sex, to
make life barely livable. There you were, finding that none
of these things work. Then you believed. Presto! your life is
filled with radiant love. Just like the New Testament promises.

(Dr.) Bill Bright clinched his case for finding it and sending
money to him as well as, or instead of, to (Dr.) Jerry Falwell
or the 700 Club. He brought on outstanding performers from
the entertainment world. He sandwiched them between
well-known figures in the world of sports. These celebrities
weren't ashamed of Jesus Christ. Not at all. They stood right
up there and said it "the way it is." They said, unblushingly,
my life was a mess, then one day a Christian told me about
Jesus Christ, and then Jesus Christ *himself* met me, and I *had*
to say yes to *him,* and now my life is both whipped cream and
everlasting.

The (Right Kind of) Wrong Kind of local churches are
flourishing. Pick any city and it is the same. The successful
Christianity and the community-locality local churches are at
the point of death or will be before the century is over,
almost without exception. But the (Right Kind of) Wrong
Kind of local churches are doing fine. They want those other
churches to hurry up and die so they can buy the building.
They need more space. Sometimes they can't wait, so they
build new buildings themselves with cash they have in the
bank.

These churches have the divine guarantee, and it seems to
be working. This is cold comfort to the other kind of, sometimes called the *mainline,* local churches. They know how it
will end.

Investigation doesn't know how it will end. It doesn't pretend to know. But investigation discovers that these other

local churches are thriving and that they ask new members
to check their modern spirits at the door, before they come
in. The modern spirit believes that a human being is self-
determining and free.[6] The modern spirit believes the end
of a human being is to struggle against oppression and to
practice autonomy. It is a tested belief. It fits hand-in-glove
with the believable. Freedom and self-determination are the
conditions for thinking about and for *being* a human being
at all. And you can check it out. They may be burdensome
at times. They impose political obligations on us all. But
human being knows itself as just this freedom and self-determination.

Investigation finds no withering critique of the modern
spirit in the (Right Kind of) Wrong Kind of local churches.
They don't have to bother. Modern people check their freedom and self-determination at the door, glad to put them
down, it seems, in the rush to get back to what for all the
world looks like superstition, magic, and ideological oppression. Religion is the opiate of the people, you say? Fine. I'll
have some, say these people. Better a little opiate than a lot
of disgusting historical pain, they say.

These other churches can succeed because they are no
longer the voices of any locality at all. Every kind of local
church Christianity has a location. It is intimately related to
its location. It proves itself by doing something to the location, or being a good tool of the locality. Local churches have
always been able to point to the difference they make in the
locality. And as a matter of historical truth, they have often
made a mighty difference. These newly successful (Right
Kind of) Wrong Kind of local churches make no difference at
all. They don't even try. They are located in television, in
radio, in commerce, in merchandising. That is their (non)lo-
cality. Their concerns are commercial. They want instant
belief in order to get instant cash. They point to their success

in unfailingly commercial terms, because it is for them primarily a commercial success. And this species of success is taken to be what the divine origin of their churches proves.

On such terms the Mafia has better credentials than all of these churches put together. It makes more money, for one thing. It doesn't report its earnings to the IRS, either. It could buy the television stations (Dr.) Bill Bright merely buys prime time on. If commercial success is taken to be the mark of divine origin and favor, then the Campus Crusade, the 700 Club, (Dr.) Jerry Falwell, (Dr.) Billy Graham, (Dr.) Ted Armstrong, and dozens of other spiritual entrepreneurs, plus all the other (Right Kind of) Wrong Kind of local churches in America *put together* aren't as successful as one large gambling establishment in Las Vegas or New Jersey. And for every single Jesus Christ–believing entertainer or sports figure these other local churches can point to as a visible mark of their success, the gambling casino can run out fifty whom it can point to as the visible mark of its success.

The (Right Kind of) Wrong Kind of local churches could make a case for being successful racketeers of the spirit, perhaps. They are very successful at superstition and magic. They might even be able to conclude convincingly that there will always be numerous people who do not want to endure the pain of present-day historical life. And these other local churches, if properly set up, can gather up these cripples. But it is neither a real nor a lasting success—nor Christianity, as Kierkegaard would have us add. They are successful at television because television is successful. With good merchandising techniques you can sell anything on television. That is what local church Christianity knows. And that is why the apparent success of these churches is cold comfort. It deepens the gloom.

The Christian Way To Get Out

Like the church's Lord, who saved the best wine till last, investigation now reveals its surprise. It is no surprise to you and me, however. We've known it all along. But it is still theoretically surprising to come upon massive evidence of something else in local church Christianity besides local church Christianity.

American feminism was born in local churches,[7] for instance. By now feminism is a world-historical movement. In America it encounters its stiffest resistance in local church Christianity. The difficulties it has experienced in passing the Equal Rights Amendment are almost all traceable to local church Christians who hate the thought of feminism.[8] Phyllis Schlafly is a good example. But feminism came out of local churches in the first place. It was born in the antislavery movement, itself born in local church Christianity.[9] Once out as an actual movement, feminism was energetically supported by local church Christian women. The founding theoreticians of American feminism—the Wollstonecrafts, for instance—were local church Christian women.[10] They were crack theologians too. That is surprising. In fact, it is bizarre.

Or take Christian socialism. It is at least as Christian as it is socialist, and both came out of local church Christianity.[11] Walter Rauschenbush and Reinhold Niebuhr both went to Sunday school. Looking at local church Christianity as steadily as we have been doing, who could have predicted anything that historically outrageous?

As with the abolitionist movement in the nineteenth century, so in our time we see strong affirmations of gay pride coming out of local churches, which otherwise hate homosexuality more vividly than any other institution in the society.

Anita Bryant is not surprising.[12] Jim McGraw is.[13] If we keep looking, we see energies for nonviolent resistance to political-economic oppression come boiling out of local churches that have been the natural home of privilege and power since Puritan theologians provided the necessary theorems for a covenant of grace.

A straight up-and-down hard Bible theologian like Richard Lovelace goes so far as to argue that the energies for quick social change in the nineteenth and twentieth centuries have come not out of local churches in general but out of specifically conservative-evangelical local churches![14] He is probably wrong about that, but it is certainly interesting that he should be trying to make the argument.

These examples are suggestive. They are weird, too. Each of these developments has vividly historical origins. They have come out of local church Christianity. That is why investigation concludes there is something more or less permanently in local church Christianity besides local church Christianity. It could be called a factor of the permanent theologically ridiculous. At the same time that local churches are bragging about having sprung out of the mind of God, there seems to be something else there springing out of the mind of history, God's half-witted Brother. Exactly when the covenant of grace is running out of gas, Christian "ecofreaks" appear, making the friendly suggestion that we use the sun for energy. They read about it in the paper, they say—meaning, of course, *not* in the New Testament.

Our contemporary experience of these novel developments is not, however, novel. It's always been that way, apparently. The church always has been spinning out more-than-church. There has always been something in Christianity and about Christianity that is permanently beyond the apostles and decidedly *un*official. It is always prescriptural. It is always ecstatically egalitarian. Robert Wilken

contends it started that way.[15] He says the Christian movement that was started by Jesus was a movement more than
and before it was a church. It was so powerful because it was
startlingly inclusive. Also it resisted the Judaistic temple aris-
tocracy in Jerusalem. These Christians made it up as they
went along.

Though more timid than Wilken, some New Testament
scholars affirm his contentions.[16] They doubt the accuracy of
the Pentecost report in Acts 1 and 2. Said another way, they
think the account is a fabrication. Said yet another way, it
didn't happen. It was apparently placed in Acts to support
the claim of the apostles to be the guardians of Christian
orthodoxy and to authenticate the claims of the church in
Jerusalem to be Christianity's home base. Against these
claims, these scholars speculate that Christianity began in the
hills and caves of Galilee without any spooky supernatural
nonsense at all. It spread from Galilee as a self-conscious
movement of religious, economic, and political outcasts. It
was prescriptural and unofficial. We know so little about it
because, obviously, the scriptures of the apostolic church
authorities have wiped out almost all traces of its existence.

That official-apostolic Christianity should look back to the
stylized New Testament history is for Wilken a double irony.
The history is really a second-century version of first-century
history as seen through the eyes of codifying, canonizing, and
orthodox successors to the apostles. The other irony is that
later successors of the apostles should consider the stylized
New Testament history as normative. And it is one of
Wilken's theses that Christian history is exactly the history of
looking back at the first century, where somehow the essence
of Christianity in its purest, most normative form will be
discovered. It is his counsel that any present-day Christianity
has developed historically and has instituted changes historically, and could better deal with its problems by looking at

its history than by scurrying to the New Testament to discover a blueprint for the twenty-first century.

Robert Wilken himself is a throbbing little portion of local church Christianity who is yet beyond it all. He doesn't go along with the official gag. He doesn't salute the flag. There are thousands like him, though not all of them are church historians. They don't buy the official program, either. As we have many times noted, they probably don't go to church. They are a part of what we have called the factor of the permanent theologically ridiculous. It is ridiculous because they are the only thing transcendent about local church Christianity; it is theological because it may actually be *the Transcendent Itself.*

Well, what comes out of local church Christianity besides its bragging about Pentecost, this "other" reality, once out generally stays out. For two reasons. It is not comfortable *in* local church Christianity and wouldn't find very much acceptance anyway. So while it continues to generate the solution, the solution keeps *leaving.* We found the same situation existing in seminaries. The solution to the problem seminaries have become to themselves keeps leaving the seminaries or, on occasion, is thrown out. Local church Christianity doesn't recognize the way out of the problem it is proving to itself. It doesn't even recognize that its problem is its vain insistence on being the only kind of Christianity there is. So how can it recognize the way out of the problem?

The problem simply is that local church Christianity will have to either give up its cover story of a divine origin or give up the ghost. As we have seen, there is a lot of resistance to giving up either one. The evidence seems to suggest that dying local churches would rather keep on dying than begin acting like a historical movement with the autonomy and sense to shape itself along lines it could suggest to itself. It generates its own way out but ignores the possibility.

We return to the once-great church to which only thirty-five come on Sunday mornings—the one that took the cram course on church sociology in order to attract new members. It looks to its own tradition for clues on how to survive. It does not consult its own experience, which would quickly reveal how many fine Christian people have gotten out or why.

Why should this church have worship services at all? Why should it have a building? Why should it think to require money of its members? Why should it have an expensive preacher? Why should it maintain such a splendid organ? Why meet on Sundays?

The same questions could be put to the small city church we described, the one just over the hill but on the way down. Neither church could accept them as real questions because what they do is given in the church tradition, itself founded in the New Testament. That would be Robert Wilken's point. The blueprint for the twenty-first century is to be found in the book of Acts.

Both of these churches are community-locality local churches. They speak with the voice of the locality and have traditionally tried to abolish the difference between Christian and neighbor. They feature themselves as the people of God in the community, which features itself as being exactly coterminous with its topography. The model isn't working any more, obviously. But the model has *always* been nonsense, Christianly speaking.[17]

Harvey Cox remembers with great affection the little Baptist Church in Malvern, Pennsylvania where he grew up.[18] Harvey Cox is now a celebrated professor at the Harvard Divinity School. He is the biggest thing that ever happened to that Baptist Church, or to Malvern, as far as that goes. Will the church consider its own experience in regard to Harvey Cox? He got away. He's now all over the world—speaking, looking, thinking. His Christian community is as broad as the world. He doesn't think of himself as a Christian citizen of anywhere, particularly not of Malvern. Why should the few people still remaining in that little church, if in fact it has not already folded, not follow his example? They are not only Christian citizens of Malvern. They belong to a much broader community as surely as Harvey Cox does. They are as capable of thought as Harvey Cox is. He doesn't go to church anymore unless he wants to or he's preaching. Why should they? He has discovered that Christianity does not depend on being located somewhere. Why shouldn't they? Harvey Cox is a socialist. Why aren't they socialists too?

The reason is they don't consult their own experience. They do not have direct theological intuitions.[19] They think experiences of the transcendent occur on Sunday mornings or when looking at a sunset or while having sexual intercourse. The transcendent is trembly, they think. Yet direct theological intuitions are available to them in their own *corporate* experience. Local church Christians could actually see in their own experience that the best things that ever happened in their churches were the people who got away. These churches have been good for *something*. So why not go all the way down that intuitive pathway? If the good of the local church is to leave the local church, then the local church could just possibly leave itself and be *altogether good.*

A theologian named John Cobb has gone to some pains to identify a "structure of Christian existence" that is historically and theologically prior to churchly existence, of which churchly existence is merely an expression.[20] Such an understanding is certainly in better keeping with the little actual first-century history we know, and, of greater importance, in far better keeping with our own lived experience. What moves us, shapes us, or challenges us may very well present itself within the context of churchly existence, but not necessarily. And these experiences do not originate in the minimal believing authoritative tradition, or the preaching that informs it. They are experiences of direct theological intuition, and they result in activities that are in that moment transapostolic, simply because they were not grounded there, in the apostles. Moreover, these experiences are grounded in contemporary realities, and the activities, associations, and insights that follow are related to the structure of these realities at hand.

I am encouraged by the history of Christianity to report that the novel, far-reaching, radically powerful events have occurred outside the apostolic authority structure, hence outside churchly existence. The historical development of local church Christianity we are made to believe is all there is has itself been powerfully shaped by events it did not initially understand and that certainly occurred outside its jurisdiction.[21]

Clearly, Edward Farley has had the last word so far on this matter.[22] He happens to be "simply"—his own most favored word—the most brilliant theologian in America. He goes John Cobb one better. He defines the historical form of Christian existence with precision and, to avoid confusion, calls it *ecclesia.* He does not want to confuse it with *church,* or *churches.* Therefore, he regularly distinguishes this *existence* from churchly existence. By use of precise, phenomenologically careful language, he defines ecclesia as an historical form of corporate existence. The modification of this existence toward redemption is experienced in relation to the divine presence. It is the experience of the recovery of what is truly and fully human. Said another way, it is the experience of being delivered from evil. Yes, to be sure this ecclesia develops a language of its own, churches, institutions, traditions, piety, a sociality, even theology. But *it* is forever more than what has developed—and deeper.

He maintains that ecclesia does not have a temple, is not a nation, or a race, does not have authoritative books and traditions that function as the necessary conditions for the redemptively working divine presence. Ecclesia has no boundaries. It is not bonded to localities. It goes sailing on through boundaries. It is a vast restoration project. What is being restored is the truly human. It is a corporate project, as it must be.

Seen in this way, churchly existence is always a temptation to itself. The temptation is to assign to itself the role of being the necessary condition for God's redemptively working presence. This is another way of saying the church is always tempted to understand itself as the Body of Christ, which it *absolutely* is not. Christian existence *is,* or as Edward Farley puts it, ecclesia *is.*

When it is thus suggested to local church Christianity that local churches leave themselves, local churches need not fear that they are leaving Christianity. They would be getting into Christianity. They would be rectifying a ghastly blunder. In losing their lives, they would find them. They would be taking the divinely appointed way out. It is so easy to do, too, as millions have discovered.

III. GOD'S LOVING PLAN

5. Forget Auschwitz!

☐ THE NEW TESTAMENT SAYS THE APOS-
TLES SAY GOD SAYS GOD IS LOVE.

By concentrating on New Testament history, we can identify a characteristic development, inevitable perhaps, but nonetheless a progression of related occurrences. First, we find the apostles preaching a gospel they certify to be the Gospel of God on the basis of their authority. This authority derives from having been appeared to by the Risen Lord and fallen upon by the Holy Spirit. By presenting just this species of certification, they attempt to ground the Gospel in an actual resurrection. This is an unsuccessful attempt, merely because the resurrection is an item in their preaching, not an event as public and indismissible as, say, the crucifixion. Second, the same apostles preach the divine creation of the Christian church, which testifies by its faith to the power and truth of the Gospel as the very Word of God. And that preaching is the Gospel. The apostles consider the church as the fellowship of believers in the Risen Lord, and once more attempt to ground the *church* in the resurrection. Again, they are not successful, because the church is the creation of preaching about the resurrection.

We are not accustomed to looking at these two developments side by side; therefore, it does not occur to us that they
are intellectually puerile and a spiritual absurdity. We might
better call them a blunder than a fraud or conspiracy, which
they could also be called with much reason. They are, in fact,
blundering attempts to find a solid divine ground outside the
history before their eyes. Without doubt, the Gospel had an
historical origin. There was a time when there was no Gospel,
then there was a Gospel, in the same way that the church has
an undoubted historical origin—both connected with Jesus,
who also had an historical origin. The blunder consists in the
literally gross apostolic attempts to substitute divine origins
for historical origins by the unbelievably simple procedure of
substituting the authority of preaching for the authority of
concrete lived experience.

The third development depends on the first two. Apostolic
legatees, the second generation in this parade of witnesses,
devised a theory of direct divine inspiration, by which means
they gained a divinely inspired book of the apostles to add to
the divinely inspired book of the preapostles, that is, the Old
Testament. This was another and more mean-minded blunder; it had the effect of setting the original apostolic blunders
in everlasting concrete. The various writings each had historical origins and were related specifically to a church and
preaching that also had historical origins. The most drastic
blunder substitutes a divine origin of the writings for the
historical origins.[1] Preaching and the church ever after are
driven by sequential apostolic authority to find their origins,
their meaning, their self-understanding in a *Holy Bible*,
where the church defends the divine origin of the Gospel,
and the Gospel defends the divine origin of the church.

Substantial matters of mere truth arise instantly. Historical
questions fairly beg to be asked. A species of these questions
is directed at the very beginning of what the New Testament

calls its history. Pentecost. This event was reported on apostolic authority to have occurred. The report appears in a
document written not fifty days after the ascension, when it
is reported Pentecost occurred; it was written fifty *years*
later.[2] To consider these questions would, however, distract
us. By now we recognize the importance attached to divine
origins, but in just such a way that we do not recognize the
divine *being* everywhere said to have founded the church,
preaching, and scripture. Wanting to think well of God, and
perhaps worship him, we should nevertheless look at the
number-one theological issue of the concrete God who develops parallel to apostolic preaching.

For all the preaching about love, grace, reconciliation, and
fidelity, the apostles are, as we have seen, always preaching
about God, the very God whose offering of grace is condi-
tioned on his demand that human beings undergo a specific
experience of acceptance-conversion-faith. After that experience God gives the grace, and continues to preserve what
has all along been a priceless belief of his: that there are
special peoples he chooses to elect. We recall that this God
patiently stores up the vengeance of eternal destruction for
the human beings who do not have the required faith experience. With this God it is "Believe and you shall be saved," or
else. Those human beings not chosen to believe, which is to
say, not elected, *don't* believe and are damned.

This is the God who speaks and speaks and speaks. We
should be wary of considering his much speaking a mere
metaphorical way of putting the situation for fear of inviting
heavenly wrath. It is actual speaking. Human beings hear
God speaking and know it is his word. They have *conversa-
tions* with him. But whenever and however God speaks, he
does always institute an authority to speak further about
what he has said. He wants it that way. He does not like to
speak to everybody, since the evidence is overwhelming that

he does not like everybody. He prefers his selected authorities to *preach* to everybody.

This God has a particular fondness for suffering and death, apparently.[3] He thinks all people deserve suffering and death because they are sinners. He knows they are sinners because they do not obey his law-words authoritatively delivered by Moses. It makes no difference that some human beings have never heard these law-words. They know in their hearts, God has seen to that. When human beings suffer and die because they are supposed to and deserve to, God is merely satisfied. When his Son and his Son's friends suffer and die by their free choice without either deserving to or needing to, well, God is delighted and happily cancels some deserved suffering and dying due *their* friends.

This is a mighty God. He rules everything. He sends his Son to the world, arranges to have the Son killed but promptly raises him from the dead, then establishes faith in the risen Son. Faith can see that God has an absolute but absolutely mysterious grip on the world's affairs. Outside the realm of his Son, his sovereign rulership is opaque to ordinary human eyes, and sometimes even to faithful eyes. Although his authorities boast inordinately of his power and justice, ordinary human life cannot see that his rulership amounts to much. Wars continue; the just perish; the unjust prosper; wickedness flourishes. But, of course, ordinary human life hasn't the faithful eyes to see that God is powerful and just but is *waiting* for the right time to bring the old era to a smashing end. His authorities insisted that it would happen in their lifetime, twenty centuries ago, and it didn't—for which God should be blamed and not his authorities, but perhaps not so much blamed as further adored for having changed his mind about when he will step in and finally triumph over ordinary human life and its sloppy sin, injustice, starvation, political iniquity, strife, repression, meanness, bigotry, lying, and death, death, death. Sometime he will stop it all; when he gets around to it or when he has seen enough.

In the favored words of his favorite spokesmen, this God is "the Father of our Lord Jesus Christ," which he may well be, as well as being the Boss and a Monster. We come to this description of God, it should be recalled, through description of the blunders that created him. While history and reason are deeply offended parties to the apostolic blunders and have ample grounds to sue, infinitely, the most aggrieved party to their blunders is God, who, we may take it, does not sue. Monster or not, Christian faith with good heart believes in a good and loving God, who sent an angel to whisper in Mary's ear the good news that she would soon be having a Jesus, and so on. Christian faith is a species of believing, simply:

☐ THE NEW TESTAMENT SAYS THE APOS-
TLES SAY GOD SAYS GOD IS LOVE.

This will be recognized as official-apostolic Christianity's third basic self-understanding. Even in its simple primordial form it is astonishingly contemporary. It still believes God is love. When investigation isolates this self-understanding, it appears God may be a big Boss, and a Monster at that. But ordinarily it is never isolated. That is what makes investigation so difficult—and necessary.

The Plan Was Good, But . . .

"God is love" is theological code for everything else. God, the sovereign creator of the universe, its sustainer, provider, judge, and redeemer *is* a fountainlike source of love, and himself loving. Christianity says the New Testament says God is love, but, more, that God has said as much about God.

Within the three basic self-understandings there is an un-

derstanding of God's revealed being that is inseparably interdependent with the understanding of the divine primacy of
preaching and the understanding of the divine origin of the
church. Put it this way: Contemporary official-apostolic
Christianity *is* its understanding of God's love. It understands that God's love will triumph over all hatred, sin, death,
unbelief, and the devil. It is certain of that. Jesus said as
much. He said, "I will overcome."

There is a routinely aggressive assurance in official-apostolic Christianity. God is running the universe. Christianity
has been assigned a crucial role in the plan. There is a plan
all right. It is called God's purpose; more often, God's will.
The plan is to overcome sin with love. While official-apostolic
commentators do not claim a detailed knowledge of the plan,
they are sufficiently confident of the overall direction to
speak authoritatively when perplexing events occur,
whether Aunt Lydia's death or the death of six million Jews.
That is one of the things Christianity is good for: It can explain things. The commentators may not profess to know
exactly what was on the divine mind, but they are filled with
assurance that the events have a loving reason. Sometimes
they seem to know the loving reason.

Richard Rubenstein visited the Rev. Dean Heinrich
Gruber in 1961. Rubenstein is an American Jewish theologian.
Gruber was a Protestant churchman who had actively con-
tested the Nazi "final solution." For his witness he was in-
terned in a concentration camp and treated like a Jew. He
was no ordinary German Christian. That is why Rubenstein
sought an interview; he wanted to talk to so loving a churchman. Rubenstein asked him, "Was it God's will that Hitler
destroyed the Jews? Is that what you believe concerning the
events through which you have lived?"

Gruber responded with scripture, a portion of Psalm 44:22:
". . . for thy sake we are slaughtered every day. . . ." He didn't

like the slur on God's majestic love that Rubenstein's question seemed to contain. God's love can handle death, can *demand* it. Gruber continued into a personal reflection:

> When God desires my death, I give it to him! . . . When I started my work against the Nazis I knew that I would be killed or go to the concentration camp. Eichmann asked me, "Why do you help these Jews? They will not thank you." I had my family; they were my wife and three children. Yet I said, "Your will be done even if You ask my death." For some reason, it was part of God's plan that the Jews died. God demands our death daily. He is the Lord, He is the Master, all is in His keeping and ordering.
>
> At different times . . . God uses different peoples as his whip against his own people, the Jews, but those whom he uses will be punished far worse than the people of the Lord. You see it today here in Berlin. We are now in the same situation as the Jews. My church is in the East Sector. Last Sunday I preached on Hosea 6:1 ("Come, and let us return to the Lord: For He hath torn, and He will heal us; He hath smitten, and He will bind up"). God has beaten us for our terrible sins; I told our people in East Berlin that they must not lose faith that He will reunify us.[4]

While Dean Gruber did not speak for a church body, he spoke official-apostolic Christianity. God does not stop being love or give up running the universe when the going gets tough. He gets going. Therefore, as Nebuchadnezzar had once been used by God as a whip of chastisement against the Jews—a clear biblical precedent—so the Nazis had been the rod of God's righteous anger. The Jews had sinned. They were punished. This may seem a very stern love, but it is love nonetheless.

Similarly, Germany was being punished for its crimes against the Jews, in the Dean's eyes. Love triumphs again.

Rubenstein was appalled by his conversation with this noble representative of Christian faith. He could not believe his ears. Since he did not stand within the Dean's theological

circle, Christian explanation sounded pretty blood-thirsty.[5] It
sounds that way to a lot of official-apostolic commentators
too. They are hypersensitive to this particular explanation
because it has become such a problem to them, or, better
said, awakened some fundamental uneasiness in them. They
can manage Aunt Lydia's death easily. They put her in a
coffin and say prayers of thankfulness. She was a good Christian woman, they say, and she is in heaven by now. But six
million Jews killed by deliberate rational design is another
matter. It has them worried, no matter what the New Testament says.

On the whole, official-apostolic Christianity does not profess to be as clear about Nazi atrocities as Dean Gruber is. Its
basic profession is "We don't know; it certainly is a mystery."
But then it adds, significantly, "God did not will Auschwitz."
This is subtly argued by a philospher-theologian named John
Hick. He says God did not will, permit, or allow Nazi atrocities.[6] So what can be made of them?

> First, as regards the millions of men, women, and children who
> perished in the extermination programme, (our Christian aware-
> ness) gives the assurance that God's good purpose for each indi-
> vidual has not been defeated by the efforts of wicked men. In the
> realms beyond our world they are alive and will have their place
> in the final fulfillment of God's creation. The transforming impor-
> tance of the Christian hope of eternal life—not only for oneself
> but all men . . . is vitally relevant here.

Translation: "So, the Jews got theirs on the other side."

> Second, within the situation itself, the example of Christ's self-
> giving for others should have led Christians to be willing to risk
> their own lives to help the escape of threatened victims; and here
> the record is particularly good but also, unhappily, in too large
> part bad.

Translation: "So, the Jews *could* have been aided because the Christly example is after all available to Christians in such abundant measure that it can be used as a positive vindication of God's honor. It is, of course, regrettable that so few Christians took advantage of the Christly example. For that blame Christians, please, and not the example-giver."

Third, a Christian faith should neutralize the impulse to meet hatred and cruelty with an answering hatred and cruelty. For hatred begets hatred and cruelty begets cruelty in a downward spiral that can be halted only by the kind of sacrificial love that was supremely present in the death of Christ. Such a renouncing of the satisfaction of vengeance may be made possible to our sinful hearts by the knowledge that the inevitable reaction of a moral universe upon cruelty will be met, within this life and beyond it, without our aid. "Vengeance is mine, I will repay, says the Lord."

Translation: "So, Christian faith stays the hands of any outraged humanists and Israeli thugs seeking to avenge the deaths of the Jews. And this, too, is the work of God, sparing the Nazis."

Hick's conclusions are more nearly the official-apostolic Christian view of the matter. It blames German Christians. If Jews have a complaint, they would better lodge it with the church than with God. The plan was good, but there was a breakdown in its execution.

But herein lies the tiny germs of uneasiness. What kind of plan is it that breaks down with such terrifying results? If theological reason can muster up that kind of explanation, it can't stop going on to the next question. It has chosen to explain and there is more to be explained. What is the sense of calling what happened a *plan* or a *loving* plan? Jurgen Moltmann, among the few German churchmen to have addressed his countrymen's genocide openly, says God was

brokenhearted by the whole thing. *This* shows his love.[7]
Rosemary Ruether says that attending to God's brokenheart-
edness didn't do a lot for the Jews, and did them in in the first
place.[8] John Wild sees this as a huge theological explanation
thrown up to protect God's love from attack. And Wild sees
the critical importance of twentieth-century radical inhumanity, signified by Nazi genocide, for steady-as-you-go,
business-as-usual theology.

Wild throws down the challenge. He says, unequivocally,
"God is not responsible for Hiroshima, Buchenwald, and
Auschwitz." And Wild knows who is responsible. Human
beings are. And a part of what they are responsible for is
creating a plan and then calling it a divine plan. Obviously,
he is not an official-apostolic thinker.

> [Man] is free to become inhuman and to inflict untold agonies and
> even annihilation upon himself and others. He is also free to
> recognize his guilt, to take it over responsibly, and to organize a
> more human world. But whichever way he chooses, he is respon-
> sible, for he has power over the nonliving and living things and
> nature. He can communicate with his fellows and is free to inter-
> pret and order things as he wishes. No one will do this for him.
> Hence the traditional conception of a divine plan to which he can
> attribute his evil intentions and vicious mistakes will have to go.
> These divine plans are comforting constructions of his own, to
> relieve him of responsibility. They are bad excuses which have
> now lost their power. If there is any divine plan, it is that man
> should become free and responsible. If he does not do so, he is to
> blame, and in his heart he knows this.[9]

By its own internal self-understanding, official-apostolic
Christianity *knows* God is running the universe and God is
love. It has the tokens of that knowledge in the Bible, the
churchly rituals that maintain contemporary continuity with
biblical knowledge, and a 2000-year-old tradition of theological reflection. Official-apostolic Christians may (unofficially)

agree with John Wild in the deep regions of their privacy no matter what the New Testament says. It may have been their personal experience that complicated theological explanations aren't much good outside of church; in their hearts they may know that few things work for good and they will take the credit for them every time. But officially and apostolically these Christians do not, have not, and cannot agree with John Wild. They would in the moment cease being who they are.

Christianity will not concede that its divine plan is a human construction any more than it will concede the Christian church had an historical origin or that preaching originates in the consciousness of the preacher. It insists that its understanding of the divine being had a divine origin; it will keep a strong hold on that understanding in spite of Buchenwald, Treblinka, Hiroshima, and My Lai. Its strategy is to *forget Auschwitz* and get on with the churchly business.

The churchly business has been gotten on with; in the grips of its selective amnesia, official-apostolic theological reflection has gone on with its business too, as though it had not somehow become an immense problem to itself.

By itself Nazi genocide throws into question the easy theodicy that has served theologican reflection since Luke and Paul first wrote it and apostolically certified successors called it Word of God. This theodicy has gone out of its way to provide Christianity with historical understanding. It has interpreted plagues, wars, madness, the rise and fall of nations, racial origin, sexual origin in terms of their place in the biblically revealed plan of God. This is more than theological superstition. It is more than the use of precritical reason, which is to say, the misuse of myth. It is the justification of God's ways according to a pattern of understanding developed in the Bible and extended in doctrinal and dogmatic reflection. Official-apostolic Christianity has not hesitated ordinarily to provide its specific interpretation of historical events on the basis of its unique self-understanding—of God. What then does it make of the Jews sailing into the ovens, being machine-gunned, gassed, tortured, starved, experimented with, raped, mutilated, humiliated, dehumanized? What does it make of Hiroshima? What does it make of the thousands of that unlucky city's inhabitants incinerated, blinded, consigned to slow death by radiation poisoning? Did God love *them*? It would seem, from the evidence, that God loved their murderers more. Is God's love merely in the account of that love? That is the other alternative, probably more dreadful.

Whatever began going bad in recent Christian theology, it began with the revelations of World War II atrocities. Neither the selective amnesia nor the rational technique of philosopher-theologians has quieted the anxiety now worked up into something like a big internal pressure, a problem it has discovered it *is* to itself. I don't profess to know what began going bad, but I'm convinced that is when it started going bad. I *guess* that the atrocities forced the isolation of "God is love" from its churchly and kerygmatic settings. The mere weight of historical occurrence shoved a moral consideration into the customarily ecclesiastical atmosphere where "God is love" is such a beautiful expression.

Indianapolis, Indiana

George Edwards provides a finer focus on the problem that official-apostolic reflection has become to itself.[10] He questions the complicity of the dominant conventional theology in the procedures of war at all. When German theologians and American theologians readily acknowledged the *divine* grounds for Germany and America to wage the (great) World War II, it seems to Edwards they already provided an interpretation of the inhumanity practiced by either or both sides. Presumably war is no more hell to God than to his client states. This is not a particularly subtle point, but it is ironic. The master of theological irony, Reinhold Niebuhr, was the commanding theological voice in producing a churchly consensus for U.S. involvement in the war. He argued with great cogency following the war that God surely willed the defeat of this unbelievable genocide-producing madman, Adolph Hitler.

George Edwards will have none of that "God wills war" talk, under any circumstances. God never wills war, he says. And in that understanding, Edwards drops completely out of the official-apostolic theological continuum that has made rather a specialty of justifying wars. He makes a notable point. It is that regular theology has a bellicose tendency. At least since the Constantinian era, this tendency has displayed itself in a willingness to treat particular wars as necessary, just, and divinely sanctioned. This is a further element in the problem official-apostolic theology has become to itself. It cannot speak about the unspeakable horror of Auschwitz because of its internal self-understandings and because it had previously favored the war in the name of God.

As far as dominant conventional American theology is concerned, George Edwards is an incurable pacifist. He is altogether too simple for its tastes. It understands that God is love, love sometimes requires wars, wars are hell, and had the United States depended on mere love, the German army would be patrolling the streets of our cities right now. That is Edwards' ironic point. The divine love he finds in Jesus loathes war and violence and will tolerate war under no circumstances. The divine love is not a branch of U.S. foreign policy. The premiere task of theology, he thinks, is to apply pressure on that foreign policy in order to stop wars.

Investigation discovers in the substantial churchly protest against U.S. conduct of the Vietnam War the very bellicose trends Edwards has noted. This is not a good war, official-apostolic thinkers said. We will only back good wars. And investigation discovers that Yahoo Calvinism didn't care either way. The Christians in local churches somewhere didn't like all the excitement. They expressed support or disfavor of the war on the basis of which course would sooner get the issue settled so that ecclesiastical business could get back to normal.

The response of Yahoo Calvinism to the Vietnam War issue is exactly in line with its response to the theological consequences of Auschwitz. It was significantly immune to those consequences. American Christians, in great majority, were morally deaf. They did not care. They were untouched. According to their understanding, God's love was still doing a brilliant job in their local church. Where is Auschwitz? they ask. We *whipped* Hitler, didn't we?

It was a variety of this Yahoo Calvinism that Kurt Vonnegut learned in Sunday school when he was a boy in Indianapolis, Indiana.[11] He learned it well. It provides him with a clear, dependable picture of the Christian religion. There is an invincibly powerful God who rules the lives of human beings with an iron hand; no detail escapes the divine attention. Human beings are free to do what God wants them to do. The ones God loves do fairly well; the others face eventual ruin and defeat. God obviously has favorites. Even they have a rough time of it, but everyone else gets chastened.

Vonnegut has taken this Yahoo Calvinism and stood it on its head. He calls it Bokononism in *Cat's Cradle.* Bokononist insights are found, however, throughout his fiction. And it is by way of its simple representation in fiction that Yahoo Calvinism is best understood. Characteristically, Vonnegut writes from the standpoint of God's negative favorites, the ones God has it in for. We come to understand how the Christian universe of Yahoo Calvinism would look to someone who had not been selected for the benefits of the divine love. It looks terrible.

In another place I tried to picture how this universe looks to superpoor black children in Chicago. It looks terrible, I concluded.[12]

Vonnegut never questions the Christian universe of Yahoo Calvinism. He does not subject it to a barrage of derision. He is more careful. He sees it is the earnest belief of earnest Christian people who taught it to him. As far as he can tell, it is the Bible itself that sponsors this belief. So he displays this whole Christian universe warmly. This could come from his Bokononist training—which he created. At any rate, the more careful description this universe receives, the more it appears to be a universe of science fiction and a moral disaster area.[13]

That is Vonnegut's real genius. He modulates his moral outrage from full blown complexity into maddening simplicity. Consider:

When Lionel Boyd Johnson and Corporal Earl McCabe were washed up naked onto the shore of San Lorenzo, . . . they were greeted by persons far worse off than they. The people of San Lorenzo had nothing but diseases, which they were at a loss to treat or even name. By contrast, Johnson and McCabe had the glittering treasures of literacy, ambition, curiosity, gall, irreverence, health, humor, and considerable information about the outside world. . . . That [they] were able to take command of San Lorenzo was not a miracle in any sense. Many people had taken over San Lorenzo—had invariably found it lightly held. The reason was simple: God, in his Infinite Wisdom, had made the island worthless.[14]

The literary community in America joins the theological community in groaning about this writing. They can't stand so much simplicity in one place. They prefer unmodulated, dense, labrythine-complex moral outrage, apparently. And they abhor pictures of the Yahoo Calvinist Christian universe, upside down.

Regular tenured Christian theologians especially should abhor these pictures because they bring into view the reality of churchly existence in Indianapolis. Here they are readying themselves for participation in the postmodern era and a great surge of new pluralism, while the folks at the grass roots are asking, Where is Auschwitz? Now they can get back to the Bible. Vonnegut's fictional representations are sun-clear. They show good-hearted Christian people shamelessly believing the very articulations of a Yahoo Calvinism that produces the problem that Christian theology has become to itself.

Official theological efforts to extract the Christian self-understanding of God's love from the perils historically mandated moral considerations create are heroic, no doubt, but always mocked by the reality of churchly existence. The self-understanding of God's love, when taken in isolation from its ecclesiastical and kerygmatic setting, is in bad trouble. But it is in worse trouble when it functions normally in that setting, as an interdependent part of Christianity's total self-understanding. In that setting—in the Indianapolis Sunday school room—the proclamation of God's love is almost diabolically deaf to its own moral arrogance. It must protect its normative understanding; it can't without ignoring or distorting recent history. But it is driven instinctually to interpret recent or any history. And it can't do both. That is the problem.

6. The Theology Machine

Kurt Vonnegut assumes the vantage point of a visitor from another planet in his novel, *Breakfast of Champions.* He looks at the Americans who cross his story-telling path in their functional aspect. Quite naturally, he calls them "machines." They automatically and willfully do what they are built to do, hence, what they are supposed to do. Vonnegut sees them as worrying machines, selling machines, typing machines, sexual intercourse machines, and so on. Each of these machines plays its special part in the Grand Design of the Universe. Every event has been meticulously predetermined, as both Yahoo Calvinists and Bokononists believe.

Investigation recalls this amiable whimsy and its roots in Yahoo Calvinism as it struggles for the exactly appropriate language to use in describing professional theology. It will possibly be scandalized to see itself described as a thinking machine, but as its own treasured gospel has it, the truth sometimes hurts and sometimes sets you free. The fact is professional theology resembles nothing as much as it does a machine.

For one thing, it does what it is intended to do, always, every time. According to one of the grandest conceits of official-apostolic Christianity, every Christian is a thinker, but not a top flight thinker or an always wide-awake thinker. The reason is that most Christians are absorbed with the cares of making a living and "doing mission," as contemporary theological thinkers are so fond of saying. All Christians can't be re-reading Augustine. They have work to do. Official-apostolic Christianity, therefore, has established a special class of thinkers to re-read Augustine. It pays them money to think full time about (official-apostolic) theology. And professional theologians do just what they were intended to do: they think full time about the Christian faith—as they prefer to call official-apostolic theology.

Naturally, they come to regular conclusions, as any machine does. They conclude at least once a day that Christianity *is* its origins. They seem to have to get back to those origins. Robert Wilken thinks he has spotted the event in Christian history that disposes theologians to congregate so regularly at the feet of the apostles, as though it were only ten minutes after Pentecost. This event was the birth of the act of writing church history. It occurred in the fourth century A.D. when Eusebius wrote the first church history. Wilken is fascinated because he, too, is a church historian, and also by the fact Eusebius didn't write any history.

Any historical development, any innovation, addition, or alteration away from the apostolic faith can only be a deviation. Eusibius wrote a history of Christianity in which there is not real history, for there is no place for change in his portrait of Christianity. The true church always remains the same from generation to generation, and the events that do in fact constitute the historical experience of Christianity are either the false innovations of heretics and the persecutions of evil emperors, or the efforts of faithful Christians to withstand persecution and defend the true faith against error. There is no genuine history, for there can be no history; Christianity is and remains forever what it was at its beginning. In Eusebius' history, nothing really happens—or, more accurately, nothing new happens. The history of the church is a history of an eternal conflict between the truth of God and its opponents.[1]

Although light years ahead of Eusebius in sophisticated ways to say it, what professional theology ends up saying is about what Eusebius said. There is an unchangeable Christian faith delivered straight from the mind of God through the apostles into the Holy Bible for the church to read. It is regularly unchangeable. It always never changes. Like Luther, then, professional theology can do no other; it must stand on the Word of God.

It is not necessarily disingenuous to stand on the Word of God. But theologians become almost comical when they can do nothing else with such centuries-long regularity.

Accordingly, professional theology not only comes to conclusions regularly, it gets to them in singularly predictable ways. It always thinks about itself, as though its builder had that and only that function in mind when it was built. There is a loss of integrity in the heartless modern world, you say? What does the gospel have to say about that? Furthermore, what have all the glorious fore-going others said about what the gospel says? The actual phenomena of integrity-drain soon enough get lost in apostolic space. This is a predictable procedure, whether theologians are talking about Wall Street, popular culture, seventeenth century hymnody, or the nature of homosexuality. The gospel (a euphemism for Christian faith) is simply always there, its truth mediated through the understanding of the Others, and available for use on any subject that happens to come up. It is so predictable it seems automatic, or, machine-like: whether the renowned Jurgen Moltmann (whom my publisher calls the greatest living theologian) or an absolute unknown. It is always the same.

Not only does professional theology function in these totally routine ways, it exhibits characteristics of the other kind of a machine—the kind former Chicago Mayor Richard J. Daley ran. Walter Wink called professional theology a guild, being much too kind and gentle to come right out with the more pejorative word, machine. He identified the guild as a system of friends helping each other and preserving scholarly tradition. The guild has very clear though informal rules of professional behavior, Wink said. Incoming apprentices (instructors and non-tenured assistant professors with brand new Ph.D.s) must learn the rules quickly and abide by them scrupulously or they will never make it into the guild. They make it when they are granted tenure. So, what did the guild do? It considered Wink's description a breach of professional conduct, an act of bad taste, unscholarly, and ended by refusing him admittance to the guild. It denied him tenure.

It never was a guild. It was a machine all along. Like all machines, it helps friends and punishes enemies. An enemy is anyone who represents a threat to the machine. Rude pagans or scabrous secularists are not threats to the machine, so they are not counted as enemies. Freud, for instance, no longer is a threat to professional theology and has been reclassified accordingly as a useful resource. But Mary Daly is a threat.

She has exposed the accredited, richly tenured, lusciously degreed group of pipe-smoking male theologians as something more than a machine and closer to the Mafia. Along with Beverly Harrison and Rosemary Ruether, Mary Daly is one of the three top feminist theologians in the world. What happens? Professional theology looks at a piece of apparent theological thought produced by Mary Daly. It is called *Beyond God the Father.* It seems substantial. It has the feel of scholarship about it. Daly seems to deal with evidence fairly, and she does not appear to resort to hysteria while arguing.

In fact, she seems to write pretty much as a male writer would. But she doesn't. No male would use the (male) tradition to subvert the tradition. She does this. She has a keen nose for the right place to start: at the beginning, that is, with methodology. Accordingly, she throws down the gauntlet at the beginning place:

> It should be noted that the god Method is in fact a subordinate deity, serving Higher Powers. These are social and cultural institutions whose survival depends upon the classification of disruptive and disturbing information as nondata. Under patriarchy, Method has wiped out women's questions so totally that even women have not been able to hear and formulate our own questions to meet our own experiences. This book is an effort to begin asking nonquestions and to start discovering, reporting, and analyzing nondata. It is therefore an exercise in Methodicide, a form of deicide. The servants of Method must therefore unacknowledge its nonexistence (a technique in which they are highly skilled). By the grace of this double negative may they bless its existence in the best way they know. High treason merits a double cross.[2]

We still may not be able to see why the machine would automatically consider Mary Daly, or feminist theology in general, a threat, hence an enemy. Let us look further.

Feminist theology insists at the outset that it is a theology, and not something else—weeping, tantrums, illogic, emotional discharge, political ideology, or social analysis. In order to make the claim of being an actual theology, it is obliged to display its ground. Since all Christian theologial ground is Eusebian-apostolic, hence saturated with inveterate sexism, feminist theologians go to a ground beneath the ground. They go to God before being represented as a male figure, to Jesus before a christological imperialism demanded the identification of God as his Father, hence our Father, to the church before it developed its apostolic authority system and christological imperialism, locating the whole male dominance in the divine mind.

The crucial issue that emerges from this audacious effort is the most obvious one. Is there a ground beneath the ground? Since the Eusebian-apostolic tradition gives no dependable evidence for such a ground beneath the ground, how is it known? What is it? Where is it? And here feminist theology simply fights. There is a crucial issue beneath the crucial issue, it seems, and it is the issue beneath the issue feminists want to fight before dealing with the obvious issue.

The issue beneath the issue develops around the status accorded contemporary experience. This is not immediately a philosophical issue; it is primarily a political issue. Feminist theologians characteristically argue that their experience of the reality called God in the reality called church, centered in the rituals and language associated with the reality called Jesus, is an authentic experience. It has been as subtly a female experience as a male experience of the same realities has been a male experience. The experiences are different. And they are equally experience and no more. Female experience of the core realities of Christian faith is as good as any other kind. And females do not experience the reality called God as a male reality, or the church as a male creation of a male God in which females have a secondary place, or of Jesus as a christological figure—a son.

Females have not experienced the realities of Christian faith in heaven. The determining situation of the experience has been what they bluntly call patriarchal. Male experience of the same realities is contrastable with female experience. The males in the experience, however, do not think of themselves only as participants in mere experience, they are also the featured authorities on the nature of the experienced realities. They are players and the referee. They know the reality called God is male, and is Jesus Christ's Father. They use their status as authorities to rebut alternate contentions regarding the nature of the realities. This is the controlling political issue. The female representation of their experience is knocked flat not with counterrepresentation but with ecclesiastical power.

The search for the ground beneath the Eusebian-official ground, or the finding of that other ground will therefore be viewed as methodologically impossible; furthermore, silly, philosophically vain, theologically immature, and generally frivolous—by professional theology. This is the issue beneath the issue. That's the one they fight. They fight it as a deeply theological issue, although immediately political, since it is the machine politics of professional-male theology that betrays its actual character as a machine. Feminist theologians analyze the structure of the machine as a theological analysis. They provide a detailed picture. Male theologians control the procedures of theological education. They control scholarly projects and pursuits by controlling their funding procedures. They edit religious journals. They control religious book publication. They manage religious foundation granting policies. They control access to professional teaching. They control access to professional ministry. They determine ordination policy and practice. They run the church. They control the official-apostolic tradition in which their authority is grounded. They specify and pontificate inordinately about the official and true Christian view of women, their nature, place, role. Rosemary Ruether makes a brilliant point of this in her hilarious presentation of Augustine's views—the official view. The options provided women are three: whore, wife, and virgin.[3] Theologian is not one of the options.

Of course. It could have been predicted. Mary Daly is an enemy. How could she be a theologian? Predictably, routinely, automatically, the machine grinds out its unresponsive unacknowledgement of this untheological nonanalysis.

And while professional theology will hold the door for her as she leaves the room, once she is gone, they will have many a comradely laugh about women theologians and their strange notions. It is that automatic. They will laugh every time, protecting themselves, as they must and always have, from external attack and the threat of internal ruin. Well they might.

The Modern Post-Modern World

In principle professional theology can interpret everything because it knows all it needs to know about God, God's love, and God's loving plan for the world. It has the Christian faith, after all. Professional theology may very well be able to interpret everything in principle, but it can't interpret the death of even one starving child in Bombay (or Pittsburgh, for that matter), much less all of them. Such an atrocity knocks professional theology flat. It is speechless about its God and God's love before such a spectacle. Therefore, it tends to regard the modern world as a pain in the neck.

We should keep this in mind as we observe professional theology rushing headlong out of the modern world and into the beckoning post-modern world, as it is so happily called.

There is a promising new pluralism being advocated by a few American theologians, I find. David Tracy and John Cobb are probably its most articulate representatives.[4] They see the problem theology has become to itself. They see it basically as a cognitive problem. It is technical. It is philosophical.

According to David Tracy the problem has developed because the disciplines of critical-historical analysis have blown the traditional claims of Christianity out of the water. These disciplines have developed inside Christian theology. They are not intruding aliens. The modern theologian seeks to be as open, fair, and methodologically precise as a scientist, an historian, or a philosopher. The theologian shares their secular faith. It is Tracy's general program to develop a theology that informs the secular faith. It is a service to the secular faith. He wants to write a theology that will be responsible to secularity and to the Christian faith.

John Cobb agrees with this picture and the problem description. He adds another element. He is concerned to come to terms with the presence and power of other great religions. He wants to work out a coherent theology related to these other religions. Many technical difficulties must be faced before such a theology arrives at coherence. These difficulties are largely philosophical; Tracy sees the same difficulties in his program. Both men want to work out a philosophically and theologically adequate new theism.

Both thinkers believe the time has come to produce a genuinely pluralist theology. How do they know the time has come? In their estimation the time has come because we are out of the modern liberal age. We are in a post-modern world. The modern world was the world of the Enlightenment, in which the autonomy and power of critical reason was celebrated. This world developed revolutions, science, the scientific spirit, technology, modern historical methods, sociology, scientific economics, literary criticism, critical philosophy, and liberal politics. It was filled with human beings who believed in the power and excellence of selfdetermining rationality. This rationality demystified the regular Christian universe, as it demystified the real one-and-only public universe. But it didn't stop there.

This is the crucial point for both Tracy and Cobb. The very procedures of critical rationality went further and submitted their own myths to critical analysis: for instance, the myth of self-determining reason. Freud, Nietszche, and Marx blew that myth away. So Tracy:

. . . In the examination of the modern human model by these paradigmatic post-modern analysts, Marx, Freud, Nietszche, and Kierkegaard, the cry of "illusions" is surely the most frequent and most damaging charge to the Age of Enlightenment. That charge has been expressed in a variety of ways: in Marxian terms, by the bourgeois intellectual's refusal to take no thought of or to struggle against the economic conditions which allow and enforce his privileges; in Freudian terms, by the disclosure of the subterranean forces of the unconscious which in fact motivate our presumably sure and autonomous conscious rationality; in the charges of Nietszche and Kierkegaard alike, that our primary task is not the development of a finely tuned autonomous and sincere rationalism, but the far more difficult task of becoming "individuals," of becoming a self who realizes his or her own rational limitations and possibilities and yet struggles to become a human being of self-transcending authenticity.[5]

When mystification was demystified, and disenchantment became disenchanted, the modern world, they say, came to an end. We are, they say, in a post-modern world.

Tracy (following Paul Ricoeur) calls the demystifiers of demystification "masters of suspicion." They spotted the illusions in the very critical-rational "man" who had spotted so many illusions in the Christian religion. So is it not back to square one for Christian theology? Heavens, no. Once the mythological material in the Christian religion has been spotted, Christian theology cannot pretend it isn't there. No, we can't go back to anything. We've got to go forward into the future. If we say, as Tracy counsels us, that the Enlightenment began the modern world, then that world was ended by suspicion, so we are in the post-modern world. That is the one Christian theology should go forward into.

There is one crucial difference between the modern and the post-modern worlds. The modern world has no room in it for religion. The post-modern world does, since it is disenchanted with disenchantment. Like Paul Ricoeur it yearns for a "living word."

Well, there it is, grinning at us: that dog-eared old religious a priori again, religious experience again—meaning, religious rituals (in which the meanings occur), religious traditions of meditation, preaching, the offering, the church, and the Holy Bible. Just the ticket. But this is religious experience understood in a particular way. Tracy's way of understanding calls it a species of limit experience. What a limit experience does is break the ordinariness of everyday life. We contemporary post-modern people have these experiences, just the same as all our predecessors have, and especially our first-century Christian predecessors. What makes a limit experience a peculiarly religious experience? Well, it is religious because that is where we encounter God: the limit experience par excellence. All limit experience language is in fact God language one way or another.[6]

Tracy has found a way to ground the yearning for a living word in the very stuff of contemporary human experience. But it is also grounded in first-century Christian experience, which is to say New Testament experience too. In fact, contemporary human experience has got to have the New Testament language in order to know what its true possibilities are. That is a service Christian theology can perform for these sober secular folks who are not religious at all: to show them that their quest for liberation and self-transcending authenticity is informed by the crucial New Testament way of putting things. For which we need God, Christ, and revelation.

The living word that post-modern people yearn for turns out to be—what else?—God is love.[7] And it seems that in coming to such an unsurprising conclusion, Tracy is joined by many other post-modern theologians who come at the problem in a different way but end up, happily, with the same all-purpose and thoroughly apostolic conclusion. I mean, process theologians, orthodox theologians, philosophical theologians, sociologists of religion, ex-neo-orthodox theologians, analytic philosophy theologians—the works.

Tracy's fundamental theology (to be distinguished, he adds in a hurry, from fundamentalist theology) works like a two-cylinder reciprocating engine. Contemporary experience fires and moves the piston up in the New Testament cylinder; it fires and moves the piston up in the contemporary experience cylinder so it can fire again, and so on.

In a word, demystification is followed by a re-mystification. The new mystification, suitable for a post-modern world, is limit experience language, by way of which the New Testament ground is smuggled back in, using the famous:

☐ THE NEW TESTAMENT SAYS THE APOS-
TLES SAY GOD SAYS GOD IS LOVE.

Even the super-sophisticated, encyclopedic, authenticity-seeking David Tracy is driven to end up exactly where it all started from. Christian theology is its beginning. Eusebius scores again.

Investigation finds without half trying that the modern world does not go away because some theologians yell at it. They may be out of the modern world but the modern world is certainly not out of the modern world. It endures. Much as professional theology would like to trim it down to a cognitive size small enough to allow them to stuff it into the general problem called theodicy, the modern world is not cooperating.

Just as Auschwitz refuses to be forgotten, the modern world we all know and live in continues to present spectacles of inhumanity too vast and gruesome to be ignored. Why does it go on? Whatever is God doing? Ten years ago there was a great flurry of hope in professional theology because the champion Jurgen Moltmann had rediscovered Christian hope. He exhorted Christian people to look into the future where God is and to hope in God's promises, located as they are, in the future. Ten years of that future have happened. We might as well have been looking at the past or the present for all the good looking into the future did us. Of course, Moltmann's kerygmatic assertions are always going to be theoretically true because there is always more future to look into. But ten years of looking certainly tends to dim enthusiasm that this rediscovery of Christian hope is anything more than Eusebian memorial exclamation.

Taking these ten years, no more, what has happened records inhumanities so vast that they, all by themselves, assault the entire official-apostolic Christian universe. What has happened mocks the cardinal self-understanding that God is love, in such a way that it makes little difference who says what. Love is the item destroyed. And if God does have a plan, as so many of the glorious apostolic legatees insist, then it is revealing itself to be more macabre than we ever suspected. The truth of the matter is that the horrible, painful death of just one starving child in Bombay is enough to destroy the comfortable universe professional theology lives in so confidently and in such opulence.

We learn, however, not to take professional theology's references to the world seriously; they weren't intended to be taken seriously. I can't believe confirmed secularists would be impressed with the new possibilities for self-transcending authenticity which the Christian faith is alleged to open for them. I can't believe they read theology at all, or that professional theology believes they would ever read it anyway. It is not about the world or secularity. It is about—what else? —the Christian faith. Even liberation theology is about the Christian faith, although also about liberation.

Aficionados of liberation theology's fire-eating conclusions are in fact put off by how very apostolic and official it turns out to be. It is that traditional. It is good solid stuff, and betrays no tendencies to move beyond the three basic self-understandings we have considered. It is very comfortable with them. It proclaims, well within divinely mandated churchly existence, that God is love. It has a fine sense of the elect community and its mission in the world. It is assured of the providential righteousness of God. And to suit the great heavyweights of contemporary theological thought—Jurgen Moltmann, Paul Lehmann, Wolfhart Pannenberg, and their mentor, Ernest Bloch—liberation theology is superbly eschatological. I mean, liberation theology has the Transcendent Itself constantly poised in the historical annex and liable to break into our history at any moment, according to the "paradigmatic" character of the crucifixion-resurrection. One couldn't ask for a better eschatology.

One reads the leading American black theologian, James Cone, for instance.[8] Aside from Cone's stirring remarks on black power, one could as well be reading a homily prepared by a regular white bishop or a paper prepared by a prestige-starved assistant professor of anything, anywhere. It is that cautious, predictable, biblical, Tillich-, Barth-, and Bultmann-quoting. Cone is not just inside the tradition; he has captured its center.

One reads Gustavo Gutierrez and finds a glowing love for the tradition, since he is a bishop, as well as as liberation theologian. One reads, for instance:

We must be careful not to fall into an intellectual self-satisfaction, into a kind of triumphalism of erudite and advanced "new" visions of Christianity. The only thing that is really new is to accept day by day the gift of the Spirit, who makes us love—in our concrete options to build a true human brotherhood, in our his-

torical initiatives to subvert an order of injustice—with the full-
ness with which Christ loved us. To paraphrase a well-known text
of Pascal, we can say that all the political theologies, the theologies of hope, of revolution, of liberation, are not worth one act of
genuine solidarity with exploited social classes. They are not
worth one act of faith, love, and hope, commited—in one way or
another—in active participation to liberate man from everything
that dehumanizes him and prevents him from living according to
the will of the Father.[9]

One might not hear exactly these words from the pulpit of
the First Baptist Church of Ponca City, Oklahoma, next Sunday, but what one would hear would not be outside the
domain of the bishop's words.

One is astonished, in fact, by the amount of Bible, church
history, and regular theology to be waded through in reading
Luis Carlos Bernal, Juan Luis Segundo, Dom Helder Camara,
Miguel Bonino, Rubem Alves, Camilo Torres, Nestor Paz
Zamora, and Gustavo Gutierrez. One is astonished because
these people are so much like ordinary theologians. They are
so German in their scholarly appetites, so American in their
style of studied obedience to procedure, to precedent, to
scholarly traditions; in fact, show them a tradition they have
missed, and they will gladly follow it.

But liberation theology comes to some surprising conclusions. Consider:

Messianic humanism . . . believes from its historical experience,
in the humanizing determination of the transcendent. When it
pronounces the name "God," it is referring to the power for
humanization that remains determined to make man historically
free even when all objective and subjective possibilities imma-
nent in history have been exhausted.[10]

Or:

> I have said that as a Colombian, as a sociologist, as a Christian, and
> as a priest I am a revolutionary. I believe that the Communist
> party consists of truly revolutionary elements, and hence I cannot
> be anti-Communist, either as a Colombian, a sociologist, a Chris-
> tian, or a priest.[11]

Or:

> . . .power must be taken from the privileged minorities and given
> to the poor majorities. If this is done rapidly, it constitutes the
> essential characteristic of a revolution. The revolution can be a
> peaceful one if the minorities refrain from violent resistance.
> Revolution is, therefore, the way to obtain a government that will
> feed the hungry, clothe the naked, and teach the unschooled.
> Revolution will produce a government that carries out works of
> charity, of love for one's fellows—not only for a few but for the
> majority of our fellow men. This is why the revolution is not only
> permissible but obligatory for those Christians who see it as the
> only effective and farreaching way to make the love of all people
> a reality.[12]

In liberation theology all the traditional signs are present.
But they are reversed. God loves the poor, judges the church,
scorns regular theology, hates capitalism, despises imperialism, has provisionally approved socialism, is hatching a revolutionary self-determination across the entire Third World,
including the Third World inside the United States, and has
promised to bring the imperialist United States to ruin if it
is the last thing he does. God is determined to do that. The
wages of sin is death.

But it is still theology. That's the point. Its aim, as well as
the aim of professional theology, which has dealt so scandal-
ously with liberation theology, is to stay in the theology business. And that requires somehow solving the problem professional theology has become to itself. And that requires an

honesty which investigation has learned not to expect in the modern or post-modern worlds.

Serve the Church with Gladness

As should be completely obvious by now, professional theology is far more interested in the church than it is in the world anyway. God the Father of our Lord Jesus Christ does not appear there as a monster. He is the same old loving God in church that he once was everywhere. That would furnish one big reason why professional theology is more comfortable in the churchly setting. It is, however, not the only or main reason. Karl Barth said better what professional theologians all believe. Theology is church theology; it is for the church, and for the sake of the church. It is the reflective-thinking component of the church. Were we to choose to evaluate professional theology in the same way it evaluates itself, we would look at how well it serves the church, and little else.

Professional theology doesn't sweep the floor or clean out the church's toilets. It doesn't serve in those direct ways. Mainly, it teaches the church. It has a self-conceived and self-appointed pedagogical role. It performs this service directly by teaching preachers, as we have seen in Chapter 2. That is not the end of its teaching. It writes books, articles, pamphlets, brochures, film strips, movie scripts, and conducts workshops, seminars, marathons, prayer-a-thons, and itself preaches to the church every Sunday it gets a chance —provided the stipend is right. The pedagogical goal is to help the church get the Christian faith right, then to keep it right—a hard job, considering the presence of so much self-generating Yahoo Calvinism.

It should be pointed out that professional theology has always considered itself as the church's teacher but did not do much of that teaching until seminaries began getting into financial trouble in the late 1960s. Then professional theology found this dog-eared old task lying around and was only too happy to begin helping-serving the church in earnest. Seminaries rediscovered a basic fact. The church is their employer of last resort.

However that may be, professional theology is a churchly activity always. Only churchly people really understand what it is, and they are the only ones with the least interest in the material. Professional theology performs two noteworthy tasks for the church. First, it reassures the church that the official-apostolic universe is still in place and in no trouble. God, Jesus Christ, revelation, the Holy Bible, and plenteous grace are doing fine. The Word of God is well. The gospel is still good news. Salvation is still free, and everybody is justified by faith, exactly as Paul said.

This is an undeniably important task for professional theology to perform because the church has a lot of trouble believing that whole universe is still in place. It is reassuring when professional thinkers confirm the existence of this universe and the continued good health of God. They are not ordinary thinkers, after all, the sort who haven't enough time to re-read Augustine. Professional thinkers have time to think the whole thing through and they think everything is in good shape. You can safely take it from them.

Second, in reassuring the church, professional theology reassures itself; this then doubles back as a reassured reassurance to the church. We could not easily overestimate the importance of this function. Moltmann, Lehmann, Pannenberg, and Ott teach the teachers of the church (and the teachers of preachers) how to keep the official-apostolic universe together. They reassure faith in the Christian faith, which then is of immediate benefit to what little Christian faith is left in the church.

The situation is not without irony, however. In serving the church, professional theology is also trying to solve the problem theology has become to itself. David Tracy is not the only theologian in America who has come to realize that the regular Eusebian routes to the regular divine ground for preaching, church, and theology are closed. Almost all theologians realize this. It is then with a bad faith they ignore what they know in simply retracing hallowed but exploded pathways. Few of them *simply* do that. David Tracy certainly doesn't. Neither does George Lindbeck,[13] who can be taken as a representative of a great many theologians in finding another way to solve this mighty problem that theology has become to itself. Lindbeck's way is finally Tracy's way, but it has some twists of its own we should watch.

Lindbeck can see as well as the next theologian that the Christian truth claims rest on historical quicksand. But they are still Christian and still true. Lindbeck certainly doesn't doubt that for a second. But what are their warrants? He gets at this question by redesigning theology's primary task. It is not proclamation or cleansing proclamation, he thinks. It is retrieving meanings in the Christian tradition, exactly as Moslem or Hindu scholars retrieve meanings in their traditions. Christian scholars can no longer say on their own much of anything about the resurrection, for instance, without being laughed at by the amused and the disbelieving. In retrieving meanings, however, Christian scholars are not obligated to say anything on their own. Hence, the resurrection has a meaning in the Christian tradition. It means joy, thankfulness, celebration over resurrection's theme, that God is victor over death, and so on. Fine. That is what the scholar retrieves, and presents in coherence with other meanings as the Christian faith.

The Christian faith can't be grounded firmly and satisfactorily in the New Testament historical quicksand. But it is firmly grounded in the Christian tradition. Christian people believe the resurrection. So, Christian faith is grounded in what Christian people believe. They are out there all the time finding these meanings in their rituals, language, hymns, potluck suppers, celebrations, and rites. To the question, How can it be doubted? is then added . . . that Christian people have Christian faith? Even the most cynical sociologist couldn't possibly doubt it. So, there you have it: a dandy new way to get on with the theological business.

Little wonder there is so much renewed interest in the church, in religion, and in the post-modern world where religion is rather more welcome than it is in the regular modern world so many of us still happen to live in. That is the new place these jovial Eusebians are going to as the way back to the

☐ THE NEW TESTAMENT SAYS THE APOS-
TLES SAY GOD SAYS GOD IS LOVE.

The irony does not fully appear yet. It is ironic that so much professional self-interest is attached to its renewed efforts to serve the church. But it is more ironic that this interest in the church and in the religious domain as such is so abstract, formal, and vacant. Professional theologians don't seem to be really interested. We can determine that by noting that they pay so little attention to what is actually going on in religion, or in the church.

At the same time these theologians have done their work since 1970 something else has been happening, among theological thinkers not nearly as subtle or technically accomplished, and among Tracy's and Cobb's employers, that is, local church Christians. These developments seem to fit together, and they don't seem to have *anything* to do with pluralism, new or old.

First, church leaders have begun to interpret the alarming decline of the big denominations as a Babylonian captivity.

They are not as frank as Dean Heinrich Gruber was. They do not itemize the sin, or describe the faithlessness that might have caused God to inflict these hard days on the church. They simply interpret the hard days as a Babylonian captivity—period. God is purging the church. God is preparing it for a new mission.

This is a suggestive development. The church leaders do not do a serious analysis of their churches' recent history in order to determine what has literally happened or deal with the flabbergasting reality of governing Yahoo Calvinism in their local churches. They seek a divine cause and then pronounce it, which local church Christians instantly can understand. It was God all along, they agree. Of course.

Second, fundamentalism has begun to be respectable again. It is now called conservative-evangelical Christianity.[14] It is flourishing. It has renounced the hegemony of the critical disciplines. It has reinstalled the Bible in the church as a divinely inspired, inerrant book. Conservative-evangelical Christianity has renounced the hegemony of liberal church leaders, too. Like John Wesley it sees that its job is to save souls and not to dabble in politics. Like Wesley the politics it isn't dabbling in are very conservative politics. Wesley was a royalist; he thought the American revolution was a terrible idea. Conservative-evangelicals think the *American* revolution was inspired by God, but no others, especially the Chinese and Cuban.

They are happy to see the restless youth of yesterday now eager to hear the Gospel. It is a straight, believe-and-you-shall-be-saved Gospel.

They are more than happy to see that cash is no problem either. They are loaded. Preach the Gospel, conservative-evangelicals say, and the cash takes care of itself. With this cash a conservative-evangelical empire is arising alongside the regular denominational business the level theory is trying to save. No one knows the size of the empire or the amount of cash involved because of a certain reluctance to open the books, but the cash flow is easily greater than the denominations' cash flow, and probably a lot greater.[15] With their colleges, Bible institutes, seminaries, publishing plants, books, evangelism kits, T-shirts, balloons, day-glo crosses, foreign mission efforts, television shows, healing services, speaking in tongues, workshops, rallies, campaigns, crusades, and prayer marathons, the base for the cash flow will effortlessly expand. It is fated.

Third, foreign missions has been revived as a natural American Christian activity. It was in a temporary eclipse. The big denominations were too ashamed of the expression to use it. They called missionaries *fraternal workers*. The United Presbyterian Church went so far as to rename its Board of Foreign Missions the Commission on Ecumenical Mission and Relation. In line with such a name change, the fraternal workers tried to better living conditions in foreign countries, to work with native church leaders about saving souls. The fraternal workers were eager to present themselves as helpers. Their interests in medicine and education predominated over merely saving souls by preaching about Jesus Christ. They wanted to live like Jesus Christ.

All of that temporary fraternal worker realism is now past. The *old* foreign missions have been revived. Harry Boer, a theorist of the old ("real") missions, includes this revealing testimony in his book on "real" missions:

> . . . as a missionary from India expressed it to me the other day, it is impossible for these people in their ignorance and degradation to receive our message until they are freed from the bondage and degradation in which they are kept by their heathen overlords.
>
> That is a very serious position to adopt. It subordinates Christ to conditions. Historically, it is not true. Men in those conditions have become Christians, and very good Christians too, before the

conditions of their life were changed, not only in India, but else-
where. . . . In the mission field we need to revise our ideas of the
meaning of Christian life. A Christian life is a life lived in Christ:
it does not depend on conditions. I mean that the life of a slave-
girl, a concubine of a savage heathen, amidst the most cruel and
barbarous surroundings, herself the instrument of the most vi-
cious and immoral practices, may be a truly Christian life. Christ
transcends all conditions.[16]

This nicely catches the mood of revived foreign missions
being sponsored by conservative-evangelical fervor and
cash.

The denominations had to cut back their missionary programs when faced with their various fund drains in the late
sixties and early seventies. This cutback coincided with the
revival of missionary enthusiasm, and local church enthusiasts were appalled. We give our money to support missionaries, they said, and church leaders cut back the missionary programs and increase social action programs. This was
one of the reasons a lot of cash left the denominations, and
members, too.

As a consequence there has been an upsurge of un-, non-,
even antidenominational foreign missions activity supported
by independent boards, sometimes foundations, and just
about any organization that can get the ear of local church
Christians. A withering critique of these very efforts found
them to be the churchly arm of standard American imperialism. This was what led the denominations to switch to the
fraternal workers model. The critique said the missionaries
were selling Christ as a front for Standard Oil selling kero-
sene. The fraternal workers themselves were not comfortable fronting for American business and State Department
politics.

Revived foreign missions renounce the critique, pay it no
attention. They do not *care* what American business or the

American State Department or the CIA does. They are interested in saving precious souls for Jesus Christ. They've the
cash to do it, too.

Finally, fitting uneasily into these developments, the
"human potential movement" has tried to make its way in
the church as though neofundamentalism didn't exist. It has
a different message. The human potential movement addresses the perplexing personal situation of local church
Christians with a specific message of hope. It promises some
sort of peace, definitely a renewal of dynamic emotional life,
and without doubt a revived personal religious life.

A carefully balanced view of the movement appeared in
the March 17, 1975, issue of *Christianity and Crisis* magazine.
It was balanced between the argument that the movement
isn't really Christian and the argument that the movement
is destructively privatist. The author, John Biersdorf, ac-
knowledges the possible point of both arguments, then coun-
terargues that they are not actual points. The movement *is*
Christian. Definitely. It restores faith by reuniting jittery
modern people to the deeply personal ministry of Jesus. The
author calls it the *transpersonal dimension.* Love comes
dynamically alive in the various human potential movement
techniques. Moreover, God comes alive as a (trans)personal,
knowable reality.

As to the privatism argument: Biersdorf suggests that the
movement hasn't done a lot of politics or bothered with any
comprehensive analysis of general social malaise. What it *has*
done is restore the possibility for full and knowing participation in political-social life by opening individuals to their own
depths, thus releasing their potential. It would then be assumed they would function politically and socially in humane
and dignity-conferring ways, especially toward the under-
privileged.

While it looks to be a part of the institutional reality of the church, the human potential movement is no such organization. The *movement* is a term used to describe a series of free-lance spiritual entrepeneurs who have something important to *sell* to local church Christians. Workshops are not free. Neither are sensitivity weekends. Neither are courses on meditation. The literature is not free. Nothing is free. It all costs money. Because it isn't a movement, with a headquarters and some officials, but instead is a lot of individuals and organizations making money, only the IRS has the theoretical capacity to determine just how big an operation the so-called movement actually is. It is growing. In its characteristic as a parainstitutional reality, it then must be understood as belonging to the other parainstitutional developments. And, like them, the human potential movement has hit upon a way to appeal to local church Christians, to address the substance of their Yahoo Calvinist faith—profitably.

What do we call the recent developments in American local church Christianity? Are they mutations of *real* official-apostolic Christianity? Or are they more? Are they insignificant aberrations or are they elaborations of the Christianity founded in God's love? Should we worry about them or dismiss them?

In my book *The Trivialization of the United Presbyterian Church,*[17] I dismissed the specifically Presbyterian sector of these local church developments as insignificant. I called them a "fog machine in the church basement." I was wrong. I conclude now that they are portentously significant. They are not a wave of religious enthusiasm that will soon spend itself. They are not benign.

The significance of the growing conservative-evangelical upsurge can be located precisely in its typical rejection of the modern world. I do not mean a rejection of its spirit or its authentic history. I mean a rejection of the actuality of a modern world. In this way this part of official-apostolic Christianity has simply ceased being a problem to itself. The new fundamentalism, the revival of foreign missions, the human potential entrepeneurs are in no way a problem to themselves. They know what to do; they are doing it; it is working. The way for theology to stop being a problem to itself is to ignore the modern world, pretend it does not exist.

Hence the way to deal with the internal pressure generated by historical supernaturally guaranteed divine origins is to stop dealing historically and critically. What is criticism? the new fundamentalism says. Forget criticism. In that way the divinely inspired *Book* makes a comeback.

The way to deal with ecological catastrophe, the population explosion, the threat of thermonuclear extinction is ignore them. Preach Christ. Save souls. Get in touch with your self. Send missionaries to preach Christ. That is the way to deal with the Third World and its political madness. Ignore the politics and *convert* the Third World.

The way to deal with feminists and homosexuals is to declare normative biblical truth to them about their sin.

The way to deal with Auschwitz is to forget it. The way to deal with racial bigotry is to forget it. The way to deal with Christians who can't forget is to stop talking to them. The way to deal with denominations that can't forget is to leave them. The way to deal with the bored former Christian is to purchase expensive television time and consider the unfortunate a consumer—of Christ.

This rejection of the modern world as such is not new to fundamentalism or superconservative American politics. Richard Hofstadter has contended that the two phenomena are so often found in combination because they share a contempt for the modern as such.[18] In a way, the recent developments in local church Christianity are only a bolder expression of what has always been there. But there is a definite way in which it is different.

The difference is that local church Christianity could in other times afford to reject the modern world because it didn't make any difference. The Christian universe was still in place. H.L. Hunt could afford to be eccentrically monolithic because he had a huge fortune, provided him courtesy of the providence of God. Local church Christians could dabble in religious idiosyncrasy because they were doing so well in business. And it was only idiosyncrasy.

The recent developments we have described have not occurred in that still coherent Christian universe where the modern world rejected with one hand could be taken back with the other. That universe has really fallen apart. So to reject the modern world in these contemporary times means something different. It means something more like *nihilism*. These present-day local church Christians, with their smashing Christ-filled smiles, have developed something like a classical case for wiping out everything: society, philosophy, sicence, politics, and the arts. That this nihilism wears the clothes of positive Christian declaration doesn't change its substance as a functioning nihilism.

There is the irony full-blown. At just the time professional theology gets around to serving the church and forgetting about Auschwitz, so it can do something it is really good at —religion—at just the time professional theology is regrounding everything in the religious domain, *it* begins cranking out a flat-out nihilism, with scarcely a word of recognition or approbation from professional theology.

Conclusion:
A Few Proposals

First, I propose that theologians excise the professional from their understanding of themselves as professional theologians. We don't need to hear for the four thousandth time what the word professional means, or the word profession from which it is taken. We don't need to attend to what it once meant. We don't need etymological history lessons. We all know what professional means: it means paid machine politician. Medical doctors, architects, lawyers, and plumbers may want to keep using the word. Let them. From now on, I propose theologians stop using it, stop *being* it, and in that way gain some distance from the church in order to tell the truth. The church will accept the truth about as well as professional theology has, but, finally, so what? From what we've seen of either professional theology or its churchly employer, it doesn't really make a lot of difference whether or not they accept the truth, since they already own it. It wouldn't matter in the real one and only public world. Either way.

Next, I propose that theologians get out from under the apostolic authorities which seek silently and effectively to run their thought. Theologians should run their own thought. How about some of that great self-determination for theology? A little liberty. It makes all the difference whether a theologian thinks about Peter Lombard because he is interesting and possibly important or whether Lombard is just one more respected thinker to be read. Rosemary Radford Ruether has jumped all the way out of that authority system. Her latest book, *Faith and Fratricide,* is a dramatic tour de force presentation of how to get along as an independent Christian thinker. She can do it. Any theologian can. How about a declaration of theological independence?

I propose, as Kierkegaard did, that the category of hypocrisy be reinstituted among readers of the Holy Bible as the greatest sin of all. Hypocrisy was for him the main thing to watch out for. As he so well understood, professional theologians, bishops, witnesses to the truth—ecclesiocrats all—can never be fully hypocritical because they never acknowledge the contradiction between what they are are commanded by their beloved New Testament to do and what they do in fact do. At best professional theologians can only be *sub-* hypocritical, because they get to decide what the New Testament means and what their own deeds mean—which is a pretty good racket. But for theologians it can be an important and decisive category all over again, and this not so much to honor the New Testament as to regain standing in the community of human beings as forthright participants whose words can be trusted.

In line with the last proposal, I propose additionally that theologians require themselves to honor what they admit to themselves in their basic privacy and what they admit to their close friends in intimate conversation by making sure it always gets said publicly. If what they admit in private can't be said in public, there is something badly wrong: not with the public but with them. The private domain does not need dignifying, the public domain does. It is, as Hannah Arendt has argued so persuasively, the premiere domain for the expression of opinion, since in the definition of opinion and the interplay of opinions the corruptions and prejudices of private opinion are shorn away. Public discussion is the sharp knife of criticism. Were theologians to heed such a requirement, they would reverse the present situation among professional theologians, where they articulate their basic theology among close friends and gossip in public.

I propose, not less but more, rigorous, absolutely serious intellectual work for theologians, and less faculty politics and going to church meetings. For this reason: the human race needs all the friends it can get, and serious thinking is basically a friendly activity. It helps. Robert Heilbroner's somber *Inquiry into the Human Prospect* concluded that the human race must brace itself for unheard-of and unthought-of political-economic-social realignments if the human race is to survive at all. The problems he identified with such precision in 1975 have, if anything, worsened. This is what I mean when I say the human race can use all the friends it can get. I am not proposing that theologians begin adding some of their tried-and-true Christian truths to the general human discussion of how to hold back the inevitable, as though destiny could be healed. I am proposing that in their capacity as thoughtful human beings they contribute what they can to the possibility of future life on the planet. The thinking part of theological thinking should be redignified as a constitutionally human and Christian activity.

Finally, I propose that theologians write theology from the standpoint of the mother in Bombay (or Pittsburgh) whose child has just starved to death. She would not be theology's primary reader, and her situation would not provide theology's subject matter. Her rage and grief would provide its angle of vision. With that standpoint constantly in mind, theologians would concern themselves with their inevitably technical, cognitive, methodological problems. These concerns, however, would be dominated by the event which shatters the mother's and the theologian's world. From there let the theologian write about God, Jesus Christ, revelation, holy history, new pluralism, living word, love, loving plan, righteousness, church, justice, liberation, the sacraments, self-transcending authenticity, religious experience, possibilities for existence, the Christian triumph over evil, and the resurrection. A theology written from that standpoint would have ceased being a problem to itself.

Notes

INTRODUCTION

1. James Baldwin, *Go Tell It on the Mountain* (New York: Dial, 1953); and *The Fire Next Time* (New York: Delacorte, 1970).
2. Joseph Heller, *Something Happened* (New York: Knopf, 1974).
3. Phillip Rieff, *The Triumph of the Therapeutic: Uses of Faith After Freud* (New York: Harper & Row, 1966).
4. At the very beginning I note this appearance of sexist language in the apostolic writings and apostolic traditions. I have decided in the interests of accuracy to use the sexist language that the tradition uses; it is a language I deplore and never use in my own writing about God, about human beings in general, or about individual human beings customarily referred to as *he*.
5. *New York Times,* January 5, 1976.

CHAPTER 1

1. Robert L. Wilken, *The Myth of Christian Beginnings* (Garden City, N.Y.: Doubleday, 1971), p. 43.
2. Walter Wink, *The Bible in Human Transformation—Toward a New Paradigm for Biblical Study* (Philadelphia: Fortress Press, 1973).
3. Morton Smith, *Jesus the Magician* (San Francisco: Harper & Row, 1978).
4. Thomas A. Altizer, Jr. and William Hamilton, *Radical Theology and the Death of God* (New York: Bobbs-Merrill, 1966); especially Hamilton's "Thursday's Child," pp. 87–93.
5. Jurgen Moltmann, *The Crucified God* (New York: Harper & Row, 1974), ch. 6.
6. Gustavo Gutierrez, "Praxis of Liberation and the Christian Faith," unpublished manuscript.

7. John Leonard, "Why Can't Sportscasters Ever Shut Up?" *New York Times*, November 2, 1975.

CHAPTER 2

1. The idea of a theological encyclopedia is older than the reformation, although it was among scholastic reformed theologians that it got elaborated significantly. What I mean to call attention to is the regular way in which the material theological content to be taught in a theological school is considered in any recent century to fall into the four fields we all know so well. See the article, "Encyclopedia, Theological" by G. Heinrici in *The New Schaff-Herzog Encyclopedia of Religious Knowledge*, ed.-in-chief, Samuel Macauley Jackson (Grand Rapids, Mich.: Baker House, 1953) Vol. IV, pp. 125–8.
2. Ordinarily no attention would be called to the fact that theological schools are parts of a university, since they share more with other theological schools than with universities. But the university-related theological schools have themselves been lately attempting to make exactly that distinction in order to appear more attractive—less denominational, less provincial—to large foundation funding sources. I cite in this connection an unpublished papered prepared for and with funds provided by the Rockefeller Foundation, "Working Paper on Aspects of University-Related Theological Education," written by George Lindbeck in consultation with K. Deutsch and N. Glazer. It is dated September 6, 1974.
3. The best resume of the general statistical picture is Dean Kelley's, *Why Conservative Churches Are Growing* (New York: Harper & Row, rev. ed., 1977).
4. The histories of individual seminaries and the celebrative literature they produce on various anniversary occasions contain the stories of the countless times these institutions have successfully approached wealthy Christians for money. I cite here, as illustrations, J. H. Baird, *The San Anselmo Story* (Stockton, California: The Lantern Press, 1963), and San Francisco Theological Seminary's "Century II—1871–1971–2071," produced in its centennial year.
5. Ernst Kasemann, *Essays on New Testament Themes* (Naperville, Ill.: Alec Allenson, 1964). All quotations are from this source.
6. Edward Farley, *Ecclesial Man: A Social Phenomenology of Faith and Reality* (Philadelphia: Fortress Press, 1975), pp. 3–23.
7. Farley, pp. 65–68.
8. Mary Daly, *Beyond God the Father: Toward a Philosophy of Women's Liberation* (Boston: Beacon, 1973).
9. E. M. Cioran, *The New Gods* (New York: Quadrangle, 1964), pp. 17–33.
10. Kurt Vonnegut, Jr., *Cat's Cradle* (New York: Delacorte, 1973).

CHAPTER 3

1. H. R. Niebuhr, *Christ and Culture* (New York: Harper, 1951).
2. Mill Valley, in California's fabulous Marin County, provides the setting for a deadly accurate and outrageously funny book, Cyra McFadden's *The Serial* (New York: Knopf, 1977). It will be noticed that all the churches in Mill Valley have slipped all the way out of sight as *churches;* they are simply *more* Mill Valley.
3. Winthrop Hudson, *American Protestantism* (Chicago: University of Chicago Press, 1961), pp. 81–96.
4. When I was the pastor of this church, I made a careful study of the historical documents prepared at the occasion of each of the church's many anniversaries as I prepared a document for the 135th anniversary in 1969. These documents are very clear about this church's role in shaping Chicago—a point that the pastor and members of the Church in 1969 would have been happy to withdraw, given the shape Chicago was in.
5. This marvelous statement has been attributed to William Faulkner.
6. Perry Miller, *Errand into the Wilderness* (New York: Harper & Row, 1964), pp. 1–15.
7. Miller, "The Marrow of Puritan Divinity," pp. 48–98.
8. Miller, "Marrow," pp. 48–50.
9. Hannah Arendt, *On Revolution* (New York: Viking, 1968), pp. 164–178.
10. Three good examples of this are: Lindbeck, "Working Paper;" Joseph Haroutunian, *The Wisdom and Folly of Religion* (New York: Scribners, 1940); Paul Lehmann, *Ethics in a Christian Context* (New York: Harper & Row, 1963).

CHAPTER 4

1. "A Plan of Union for the Church of Christ Uniting" (Princeton, N. J.: Executive Committee of the Consultation on Church Union, 1970).
2. The United Presbyterian $60 million, the Episcopal $80 million, and the United Methodist $100 million major fund campaigns are each one being masterminded by professional fund raising organizations. What is remarkable is that in all three cases early signs point to the possibility that they will not only make the goals but exceed them.
3. This is a most conservative estimate. For instance United Presbyterians *reported* they gave over $440 million to all causes in 1976. They gave a lot more than that, however.
4. The irony here is that denominations make money on their various food-for-the-hungry programs. They are mounted as special offerings in local churches and the denominations extract an administrative charge off the top before one penny is spent on food. As we have come to

expect, in reckoning administrative charges denominations can be extravagant in estimating the personnel and time required to administer the programs.

5. Denominational theory assumes there is a transcendent national denominational entity, as well as semitranscendent regional entities above local church Christianity. This has been a standard feature of denominational thinking about denominations since their beginnings in the seventeenth and eighteenth centuries. The theory may once have been an adequate representation of denominational facts, but it surely isn't any more, and it has been replaced by a "level" theory. According to this theory, there are administrative levels *of* local church Christianity, and these levels "support" the local effort; they should never, on any count, be considered to be *above* the only Christianity there is, the one in the pews.

6. This is a comprehensive consensus statement of the reflection of a wide variety of modern (late nineteenth and twentieth century) philosophy. The best treatment of this difficult and prolix subject is Edward Farley's article, "God as Dominator and Image-Giver: Divine Sovereignty and the New Anthropology," *Journal of Ecumenical Studies,* Vol. 6, No. 3, 1969, pp. 354–375.

7. See the monumental and classic *History of Woman Suffrage,* ed. Elizabeth Cady Stanton, Susan B. Anthony, and Matilda Joselyn Gage (Rochester N.Y.: Charles Mann, 1887). See especially Vol. I, Ch. V and XV; Vol II, Ch. XXVI.

8. *The Presbyterian Layman,* a conservative-evangelical journal, has often expressed itself in forthright opposition to the passage of the ERA. It claims to speak for as well as to grassroots Christians. The letters column shows readers in resistance to ERA too. See the April–May, 1978 issue, Vol. XI, No. 3, for instance.

9. *History of Woman Suffrage,* Vol. I.

10. See Mary Wollstonecraft, *A Vindication of the Rights of Woman* (Boston: Thomas and Andrews, 1792).

11. See Rosemary Radford Ruether, *Radical Social Movement and the Radical Church Tradition* (Oak Brook, Ill.: Bethany Theological Seminary, 1971).

12. There is no doubting Anita Bryant's origins in local church Christianity. See an "Ad Hawk" in *frying pan* magazine, June, 1978.

13. James McGraw is a United Methodist clergyperson who has distinguished himself in a variety of New York City ministries, and, even more, as Dick Gregory's collaborator. McGraw has openly joined the Gay Pride movement in the city and has distinguished himself there, too, for leadership and toughness on the issues.

14. Richard Lovelace, a preaching teacher at Gordon-Conwell Theological Seminary, has deluged friends and colleagues with numberless mimeo-

graphed unpublished essays on this subject. He promises them all that he will soon have a book on the subject which will demonstrate once and for all the truth of his historical argument.

15. Robert L. Wilken, *The Myth of Christian Beginnings* (Garden City, N.Y.: Doubleday, 1971), Ch. 7.

16. The very introduction of historical-critical methods of investigation into New Testament study admits the force of the contention. This is what modern scholarship is all about. See F. M. Grant, *A Historical Introduction to the New Testament* (New York: Harper & Row, 1963), Ch. 21, and Subert Ogden, *Christ Without Myth* (New York: Harper & Brothers, 1961).

17. I merely call attention to the marvelous irony this Kierkegaardian expression has accrued since he used it with such devastating effect over a century ago.

18. Harvey Cox, *Seduction of the Spirit* (New York: Simon and Schuster, 1973), Part I.

19. I use intuition here in somewhat the same way phenomenologists do, though without their precision. For a precise description of intuition see Maurice Natanson, *Edmund Husserl: Philosopher of Infinite Tasks* (Evanston, Ill.: Northwestern University Press, 1973) pp. 91–2. In popular and psychological usage, intuition is a kind of non- and even subrational *knowing*. Phenomenologists treat it as a part of regular *seeing*. What I mean by direct theological intuition is seeing into experiences as they are and coupling this seeing into with the sorts of theological reflection which have been the previous achievement of consciousness —in such a way that the experience has these theological elements as a part of their totality.

21. Edward Farley, *Ecclesial Man: A Social Phenomenology of Faith and Reality* (Philadelphia: Fortress Press, 1975), preface and Ch. 7, especially. I express here my appreciation for all of Farley's thought—the theological virtuosity and profundity of which has little place in a book on mere official-apostolic Christianity.

CHAPTER 5

1. Kurt Aland, *The Problem of the New Testament Canon* (London: A. R. Mowbray, 1962), argues that the actual elaborated dogma of literal inspiration of the scriptures in the pastoral epistles—II Timothy 3: 14–16; II Peter 1.19—is central to development of the very idea that there should be a New Testament canon, and, then, that there *is* one. See also Dewey Beagle, *The Inspiration of Scripture* (Philadelphia: Westminster, 1968); Bruce Vawter, *Biblical Inspiration* (Philadelphia: Westminster, 1972).

2. A. Q. Morton and G. H. C. MacGregor argue that the earliest Luke-Acts

could have been written was 80 A.D. See their *The Structure of Luke and Acts* (London: Hodder and Stoughton, 1964), p. 53. While Hans Conzelman argues the date *could* have been as early as 60 AD., he concludes it was almost certainly later than 80 A.D. See his essay in *Studies in Luke-Acts,* ed. Leander E. Keck and J. Louis Martyn (Nashville: Abingdon, 1966).

3. Consider at least one of the numerous New Testament texts which could be cited. Simply read it as though it were an inspired, hence, totally true, revelation of what God is actually like: "[Your persecution] is evidence of the righteous judgment of God, that you may be made worthy of the kingdom of God, for which you are suffering—since indeed God deems it just to repay with affliction those who afflict you, and to grant rest with us to you who are afflicted, when the Lord Jesus is revealed from heaven with his mighty angels in flaming fire, inflicting vengeance upon those who do not know God and upon those who do not obey the gospel of our Lord Jesus. They shall suffer the punishment of eternal destruction and exclusion from the presence of the Lord and from the glory of his might, when he comes on that day to be glorified in his saints, and to be marveled at in all who have believed, because our testimony to you was believed." (II Thessalonians 1.5–10.) What a God.

4. Richard Rubenstein, *After Auschwitz* (New York: Bobbs-Merrill, 1966) pp. 53–55.

5. Rubenstein, pp. 55–57.

6. John Hick, *Evil and the Love of God* (San Francisco: Harper & Row, rev. ed., 1978). All quotations from Hick are from this source.

7. Alice Eckhardt and Roy Eckhardt, "German Thinkers View the Holocaust," *Christian Century,* March 17, 1976, p. 252.

8. Eckhardt and Eckhardt; and Rosemary Radford Ruether, *Liberation Theology* (New York: Paulist Press, 1972) ch. 5 and 6.

9. John Wild, "The Rebirth of the Divine," in *Radical Theology: Phase Two Essays in a Continuing Discussion,* ed. C. W. Christian and Glenn R. Wittig (Philadelphia: Lippincott, 1967), p. 187.

10. George Edwards, *Jesus and the Politics of Violence* (New York: Harper & Row, 1972), pp. 109ff.

11. Kurt Vonnegut, Jr., of course, was raised in a home that took some pride in being agnostic. Vonnegut probably never went to a literal Sunday school in his life. But, then, in Indianapolis you needn't go to a literal Sunday school since the whole predominating culture *is* a Sunday school, or was when Vonnegut was growing up there.

12. John R. Fry, *The Locked-Out Americans* (New York: Harper & Row, 1973).

13. Vonnegut, *The Sirens of Titan* (New York: Delacorte, 1974); *Slaughter-house Five* (New York: Delacorte, 1971); *Breakfast of Champions* (New York: Delacorte, 1974).

14. Vonnegut, *Cat's Cradle,* (New York: Delacorte, 1973), pp. 87–89.

CHAPTER 6

1. Robert L. Wilken, *The Myth of Christian Beginnings* (Garden City, N.Y.: Doubleday, 1971) p. 73.

2. Mary Daly, *Beyond God the Father: Toward a Philosophy of Women's Liberation* (Boston: Beacon, 1973), pp. 11–12.

3. Rosemay Radford Ruether, *Liberation Theology* (New York: Paulist Press, 1972), ch. 7, especially pp. 99–113.

4. David Tracy, *A Blessed Rage for Order: The New Pluralism in Theology* (New York: Seabury, 1975); John B. Cobb, Jr., *Christ in a Pluralistic Age* (Philadelphia: Westminster, 1975).

5. Tracy, *A Blessed Rage for Order,* p. 11.

6. Tracy, *A Blessed,* pp. 187–191.

7. Tracy, *A Blessed,* p. 191.

8. James Cone, *Black Theology and Black Power* (New York: Seabury, 1969).

9. Gustavo Gutierrez, *A Theology of Liberation* (New York: Orbis, 1973), pp. 307–308.

10. Rubem Alves, *A Theology of Human Hope* (Cleveland: Corpus Books, 1969), p. 151.

11. Camilo Torres, *Revolutionary Priest: The Complete Writings and Messages of Camilo Torres,* ed. John Gerassi (New York: Random House, 1971), p. 370–371.

13. Torres, *Revolutionary Priest,* pp. 367–369.

13. George Lindbeck, "Working Paper."

14. This is the position of the conservative-evangelical magazine, *Christianity Today.*

15. To give an idea of the size of what we are describing, consider the announcement of Dr. William Bright, founder of "Campus Crusade for Christ," that his organization is embarking on a one billion dollar fund-raising drive.

16. Harry R. Boer, *Pentecost and Missions* (London: Lutterworth Press, 1961), p. 240. Boer is quoting Roland Allen.

17. John R. Fry, *The Trivialization of the United Presbyterian Church* (New York: Harper & Row, 1975).

18. Richard Hofstadter, *Anti-Intellectualism in American Life* (New York: Knopf, 1963); *Paranoid Style in American Politics and Other Essays*